D1020090

THE
JOYS OF TRAVEL

C.1

THE
JOYS OF TRAVEL

And Stories That Illuminate Them

THOMAS SWICK

Skyhorse Publishing

"Emotional Connection" appeared in a shorter version in *The Morning News*.
"Warsaw Redux" appeared in a much different version in *National Geographic Traveler*.
"The Place You Could Be Looking For" and "Heaven of the Bavarians" appeared in the *South Florida Sun-Sentinel*.
"What I Like About Key West" appeared in the *Oxford American*.
"My Days with the Anti-Mafia" appeared in *The Missouri Review*.
"Travels with a Book" appeared in *The Weekly Standard*.

Skyhorse Publishing books may be purchased in bulk at special discounts for sales promotion, corporate gifts, fund-raising, or educational purposes. Special editions can also be created to specifications. For details, contact the Special Sales Department, Skyhorse Publishing, 307 West 36th Street, 11th Floor, New York, NY 10018 or info@skyhorsepublishing.com.

Skyhorse® and Skyhorse Publishing® are registered trademarks of Skyhorse Publishing, Inc.®, a Delaware corporation.

Visit our website at www.skyhorsepublishing.com.

10 9 8 7 6 5 4 3 2 1

Library of Congress Cataloging-in-Publication Data is available on file.

Jacket design by Jane Sheppard

Print ISBN: 978-1-63450-821-6
Ebook ISBN: 978-1-63450-823-0

Printed in the United States of America

To Hania

My journey had taken on a new dimension and all prospects glowed.
—Patrick Leigh Fermor, *A Time of Gifts*

Contents

Introduction

We live in a visual age.

Why am I even writing this?

Because thoughts cannot be photographed.

They're not the only things.

Of all human activities, none is more associated with the visual than travel. Passport photos. Window seats. Sightseeing. Observation decks. Scenic overlooks. Open-roof buses. Glass-bottom boats. Art museums. Postcards. Vacation videos. Road movies. The Travel Channel. "The Last Time I Saw Paris." The *National Geographic* photographer. *1,000 Places To See Before You Die*. Your Best Shot. For years, *The New York Times* Travel section ran an end-page essay, then it was replaced with an end-page photograph. A tourist traveling without a camera is as unimaginable as a teenager drinking nonalcoholic beer. What would be the point? Where would be the proof?

When I was first asked to travel with a video camera, during my waning days as a newspaper travel editor, I resisted. My argument was that filming an encounter changes the dynamic; people act differently—less naturally—when they know their words and actions are being recorded. I never even used a tape recorder; I jotted down conversations in a powerless, innocent-looking notebook.

I did take photos, often of people, but not the ones I interacted with. I always thought that to be invited into someone's home and then to whip out a camera would be the height of rudeness. It would not only destroy the mood, it would firmly establish the wall between tourist and local that the locals, by their kind invitation, had graciously tried to dismantle. It would treat people as objects, no different than their city's buildings, monuments, and statues.

Unless of course they started snapping pictures themselves. You don't have to be a tourist to love souvenirs.

So let's say you do take out your camera or your smartphone, everyone spends a couple spectral minutes mugging. The pictures will capture a certain bonhomie; but there will be nothing in them of the astonishment, gratitude, or privilege you feel on having made a connection, on having entered into the life of the place.

This is not to denigrate photography; as an art, it's capable of conveying deep and complicated emotions. Rather, it's to elevate travel, whose greatest gifts elude the camera.

Joys

Anticipation

Not just unphotographable, anticipation frequently goes unacknowledged, or at the least, unappreciated. Still, we are all familiar with it: the thrill of picking a destination, singling out a country, a city, or an island, and then picturing ourselves there, unburdened and happy. We start the countdown to our departure. We now have someplace to look forward to.

Anticipation is rarely idle; it inspires us to act and then grows as we do. The Internet gives us links upon links that lead seemingly into infinity, while in a more traditional snowballing, guidebooks—after listing the sights and hotels and restaurants—recommend other pertinent books.

As soon as I dream up a trip, I plan my reading accordingly. In fact, when I have no trips upcoming, I have a hard time deciding what to read. The world—and my condo—are so full of books it's extremely difficult to settle on a few. If travel expands our experience and broadens our minds, the *anticipation* of travel helpfully narrows our reading list.

For without any borders, where do you begin? People who were good students in college often stop reading after graduation. Not because they don't enjoy it, or because they don't have time, but because they no longer have a syllabus. They stand paralyzed before the ever-growing abundance of books.

They need to plan a trip.

Before departure, I read as much as I can about where I'm going: travel books, biographies of native sons and daughters, memoirs, poetry, novels, which give more than information; they provide background, atmosphere, substance, insight (as well as topics for upcoming conversations). Because my reading tastes lean toward nonfiction, there is now a growing group of novelists whose works would have remained unread by me if not for my frequent flyer status.

One such writer was Giuseppe Tomasi di Lampedusa. I was going to Sicily for the first time, so before the trip I visited my local library and took out *The Leopard*. My response to the novel was probably different from that of most readers; I was less interested in the romance of Tancredi and Angelica than I was in the descriptions of Palermo. I picked up my pen and copied into my notebook passages like: "It was the religious houses that gave the city its grimness and its character, its sedateness and also its sense of death which not even the vibrant Sicilian light could ever manage to disperse." The travel writing of a (gifted) resident.

If asked to play a word association game with countries I've visited, I would, for many, utter the names of writers (not always native) who seem synonymous with each place: Egypt—Mahfouz. Turkey—Pamuk. Colombia—Márquez. Uruguay—Galeano. Trinidad—Naipaul. St. Lucia—Walcott. Malaysia—Burgess. Croatia—West. Portugal—Pessoa. Canada—Munro. They are literary consuls; their works sublime, essential field guides.

There are countries that, visited for the first time, allow for hours of enjoyable rereading. During one well-traveled period in the nineties, it seemed that every place I went—Mexico, Haiti, Vietnam—had served as the setting for a Graham Greene novel. Like many Americans, I dream of someday driving cross-country, and the pleasure will be two-fold, as I'll return gratefully to the pages of *Lolita*.

There are places, on the other hand, that inspire me to finally tackle classics I've long avoided. I read *Crime and Punishment* a number of years ago only because of an upcoming trip to St. Petersburg. (I had been put off Dostoevsky by *Lolita*'s creator, a fellow Petersburger who found him melodramatic.) Before a trip to Greece I not only read *The Iliad*, I audited a course on it at a local university. (A move I highly recommend; when I read *The Odyssey* on my own I didn't enjoy it nearly as much—and it's a travel book!)

Some places introduce me to books I never would have read because I never would have heard of them. One summer I plowed through Shimazaki Tōson's 750-page novel *Before the Dawn* because it is set in a town—Magome—that I was going to hike to that fall while visiting Japan. The book was not a stylistic delight, but it was informative about the mountainous region—the food, the customs, the old Kiso Road—and the period of Japan's opening up to the West.

If I'm traveling in the US, I try to find a local Sunday newspaper before my trip. I can read it online, but then I miss a lot, like the advertisements, which are far less generic than the news (fire, car crash, missing child). I read not just to learn of shows I might catch when I'm there (the Entertainment and Lifestyle sections serve the traveler's needs best), but to see ads for things that are specific to the place. Before a trip to New Mexico, I read the *Albuquerque Journal* and found a half page of notices for New Age groups. (Had I been into crystals, I would have been ecstatic.) In South Florida, the alternative weekly is ripe with ads for breast enlargement and liposuction.

Much of this reading, of course, is the prep work of a travel writer. But non-writers have introduced me to other, equally worthwhile acts of pre-immersion. When I was living in Warsaw in the late seventies, I met the American ambassador's secretary at a party—a woman from Trenton, New Jersey—who told me that before taking up her assignment she had spent hours listening to Chopin. Music is more accessible than literature while often being similarly imbued with a nation's spirit. (Certainly the case with Chopin's mazurkas and Poland.)

While traveling around Turkey in 1997, I hitched a ride with a mother and daughter from New York City who, months before their trip, had rented a selection of Turkish films. So when they arrived in the country their heads were not contaminated by scenes from *Midnight Express* (the fate of far too many Americans) but filled with the stories and sensibilities of native directors.

Also, watching Turkish movies they had heard the unintelligible, unfathomable, and transporting words that would soon be filling their ears. They gleaned something about the texture of everyday life while familiarizing themselves with the rhythms of the language, a useful visual and aural warm-up.

If you have the time to study it before your trip, the language goes from being just a gateway into a culture (as it was in school) to a living thing—a soon-to-be-deployed tool for finding your way, literally and figuratively. You commit key words and phrases to memory with the heady knowledge that very soon you'll be putting them to use. Unfortunately, this doesn't necessarily make the memorization easier, but it does add to your growing anticipation.

The Germans have a word for this feeling: *reisefieber*—from the words for "journey" (*reise*) and "fever" (*fieber*). It is one of those incomparable German abstract nouns that capture feelings shared by many people who are saddled with languages incapable of describing them. *Schadenfreude*, and the much warmer *gemütlichkeit*, are two others.

That the Germans have a word for the excitement one feels before setting off on a trip seems only natural since they are quite possibly the world's greatest travelers. They have a joke that seems to confirm this status. Three Germans are discussing their upcoming vacations. One says he's going hiking in the Himalayas. Another says he'll be backpacking around Patagonia. The third announces he's staying in Germany, to which the first two respond: "Snob!"

German travelers are avid, knowledgeable, undaunted, and ubiquitous—showing up in the most isolated places with unnerving predictability. There are numerous theories on what differentiates travelers from tourists; Paul Theroux has said that the former don't know where they're going while the latter don't know where they've been. I've always considered the difference to be more in how one travels than in where, though I would recognize as a traveler anyone who goes someplace and doesn't find a German.

Several years ago in the Cook Islands, I met a German professor who was traveling with his wife and two grown daughters. (I pictured him back in Heidelberg telling friends casually of the upcoming family vacation in Aitutaki.) Over lunch, I asked him about his compatriots' fascination with travel and he attributed it to Goethe, whose *Italian Journey*, he said, had shown the nation the value of discovering what lies beyond its borders.

It's evident in the language—which gave us not only *kindergarten*, but *wanderlust*. Long before there was a gap year, there was a *wanderjahr*. German even has a word for the opposite of homesickness: *fernweh*, the yearning for elsewhere that haunts one while home.

Long ago I realized that if I was feeling low, as if life no longer held any interest, it was because I had no trips planned. (Which of course also meant I had nothing to read.) I discovered that as soon as I purchased a plane ticket—even an intangible e-ticket—my spirits would lift at the turning of my *fernweh* from a depressant into a boon. If French is the language of love, German is the language of travel.

At the very least, it's the language of pre-travel—that innocent, blissful period before departure. Anticipation is to a journey what infatuation is to a romance: an uncritical but crucial prelude to reality. It helps us look past the coming discomforts, frustrations, embarrassments, and disappointments that might otherwise keep us at home. Because guidebooks and travel magazines never show them, we don't imagine garbage dumps, power stations, or wild-haired men shouting expletives in train stations. Destinations are depicted in a pristine or, sometimes, colorfully decayed state, and the natural assumption is that our stays in them will be equally flawless or picturesque. Anticipation of travel is always more idyllic than travel itself.

Of course, if in preparation you read the right books (i.e., literature), no destination will appear untarnished. Great artists have an aversion to clichés—like the concept of paradise on earth—that bad travel writers live off of.

You can also temper the romanticizing by talking to people who've lived where you're going. (The waiters at your local ethnic restaurant can be a good source.) Immigrants may be bitter, homesick, or conflicted, but they're insiders who've seen their country from the outside (an illuminating privilege). Also, they may have a cousin who wouldn't mind meeting you.

I tell everybody I meet where I'm going, not just to learn about possible contacts (though that's half the reason) but also to hear reactions, experiences, prejudices. I want to know what people think. If someone has harsh criticisms, I take them personally. I've associated myself with this place now, and its flaws—flaws definitely more than virtues—seem somehow to reflect on me. (Guilt by reservation.) My enthusiasm is dampened. I try to remind myself that the perceived faults could be, especially if voiced by people who've never been there, the result of false stereotypes. This idea fuels my desire to visit, for only by being there will I be able to discover the reality of a place. People occasionally have moral objections to your trips: Go to Myanmar and you're supporting the military dictatorship, they said for decades; travel to Cuba and you're breaking the law (or at least were for many years). Then you go from being excited to being defensive. But it helps you examine, in a way you might not otherwise, the motives and consequences of your traveling.

If people are envious, and tell me that the place I've picked is great, or that they've always dreamed of going there, I'm not as encouraged as you might think. What if I'm disappointed? I wonder. Will it be my fault?

If someone is puzzled—"Huh? Why you going there?"—I think: This could be good. Often, the less glamorous the destination, the more rewarding the journey.

This is the theory of a writer, someone looking for a story. Although I think some other people (like the German in the joke) enjoy not just being different, but discovering the overlooked. Many of my most fascinating and gratifying trips have been to places that had people wondering why I chose them: Vietnam in 1994 (before our government had reestablished diplomatic relations); Croatia in 2000 (five years after the war); Iowa (a continually rich and untrampled crop of Americana); Texas (which nearly qualifies, in size and mindset, as a separate country). Just reading up on unsung places (there are fewer books, but they're usually not checked out), I initiate a bond in a way that's impossible with countries like France or Australia or China. Large nations belong to everybody, while Paraguay, Latvia, Laos can be—or at least seem to be—yours alone.

Jan Morris saw places as reflections of herself, and no city was more so, she felt, than Trieste; the book she wrote about it, *Trieste and the Meaning of Nowhere*, she thought of as an autobiography. It seems an extremely idiosyncratic, and solipsistic, approach to travel, yet it's one that I share, making us perhaps part of a small minority. Studies have shown that the vast majority of sports fans, when they have no favorite, will side with the underdog because that is how most of us think of ourselves. A visit to any bookstore travel section, bursting as they all are with titles on Italy and France, reveals that this same identification with the little guy doesn't extend to travel. Just because we may sympathize with underdogs doesn't mean we want to spend our vacations in them.

It is difficult, for instance, to find travel books on Poland, which is what I was looking for in 1978. (I had fallen in love with a Polish woman I'd met in London and was planning to join her in the fall in Warsaw.) There were history books and political books, but not much else. I wanted something that would give me an idea of what to expect in terms of culture, customs, everyday life. For climatic and geopolitical reasons (an overcast country behind the Iron Curtain) Poland had not been gifted a Gerald Brenan as Spain had been, or a Lawrence Durrell as the Greeks had gotten.

I was house-sitting the summer before I went to Poland for friends in Princeton, New Jersey, and spent many afternoons in Firestone Library (in those days open to the public) reading Polish literature in translation. It was a challenge, one that frequently sent me for relief to the nearby stacks holding the Russians—Chekhov, Gogol, Nabokov—who seemed to speak to the world, and often with a beguiling lightness of touch. Polish writers were heavy, at least the ones I was reading, and obsessed with Poland; they had created a literature that required a thorough knowledge of the history. I would soon come to understand their obsession, and even share it, eventually connecting with Poles through their feeling of inferiority, their gift for self-deprecation, their fine sense of irony. But at the time, my obsession began and ended with Hania.

Then one August afternoon my parents drove me across the state to Kennedy Airport—my skeptical father at the wheel, my anxious mother beside him, and me in the backseat, their doubting, jittery offspring. Two things kept me from saying "Let's turn around": love and the commanding prospect of adventure.

When I was a child, the only time I had trouble sleeping—apart from Christmas Eve—was the night before a trip. A class outing to the Hackettstown Fish Hatchery or a family vacation to the Jersey shore would produce in me the same perverse insomnia, which prolonged my conscious anticipation but deprived me of sleep prior to an activity that called for clear-eyed alertness. In retrospect, I see that it was good preparation for jet lag.

Pure excitement, untouched by concern, was what kept me awake. In those days my trips were worry-free; I was in the hands of others, relieved of all responsibilities. One of the last of these was a high school trip to Italy with the Latin Clubs of New Jersey. It was my first time on an airplane, and I stared out the window at sunrise over the Alps—a view that was unprecedented, epic, and uncluttered (I see now) with thoughts of negotiating with cabbies and finding a hotel. Everything had already been arranged for me, and though the trip put me off package tours for life, it showed me their attraction for many: They allow you to become a child again, cared for and watched over. They give, at least to people who have no fear of flying, a smooth, untroubled prelude to the trip.

Four years later, a nascent college senior, I flew to London with the hope of finding a job for the summer. In the days before my departure I experienced for the first time the uncertainty and anxiety that travel can produce. I had no leads for a job and no names of people to contact for one. I also, uncharacteristically, had no idea where I was going to stay, or even sleep the night of my arrival. In the space of four years travel had become a serious proposition. Although I didn't think of it in this way at the time, it was good experience for someone heading toward graduation and ejection into the real world. That trip was destined, whether or not I found a job (which I did, selling Bath buns and scones in a food hall on Oxford Street), to give me a foretaste of life beyond school.

Now my trips are not such commitments. Like most people's, they don't last a summer and they don't involve work permits. But I still, usually, travel alone (unlike most people) and I'm still not good at making reservations. I'll book a hotel for the city I'm flying into, but after that I prefer to improvise. I say that I don't like being held to a schedule, and it's true. The neighborhood in which I plan to spend three nights could be dodgy, and someone there might tell me about a lyrical town in the south that I've never heard of. (As was the case, one December in Ecuador, with Quito and Cuenca.)

I think a part of me also enjoys the sketchiness, the modest risk, the stark unknown of unstructured travel because it ties me, tenuously, to the traveler I once was. It's surely responsible for my waning enthusiasm as a trip approaches. I'm usually still reading, now rather frantically, like a student cramming for a final in a course he's neglected all semester. At least one book will go into my carry-on.

But far more disturbingly, I develop a powerful attachment to home; in fact, I become the world's happiest homebody. My quotidian routine, which numbed me into escape, now seems awfully pleasant. In the TV program I see big games I'm going to miss; on the calendar, dinners and parties. Life—my life!—is going to go on without me, especially since Hania is staying, and will pick up the mail, water the plants, get invited over by sympathetic friends and neighbors who, out of politeness, will ask about me, but once that's out of the way the evening will proceed as if I don't, and perhaps never did, exist. To travel is to show your sad inessentiality.

It is in this frame of mind that, the night before leaving, I pull out my suitcase. Packing helps; I fold my favorite shirts and picture myself wearing them down fashionable streets and across stately plazas. I often place a sport coat on top, and a tie—a vintage Rooster picked up most likely on a trip to some American city with good vintage clothing stores. A tie is to the urban traveler what a penknife is to the nature lover, and the closest I get to a tool or a talisman or a hot sauce without which I refuse to travel. Then I lock the suitcase, stand it upright, and gaze in awe at its ability to house everything I need for three weeks.

Well, almost everything. My bookbag fills with my pens, notebook, passport, books (homework), and back issues of magazines I've been ignoring for months. A magazine you subscribe to helps personalize an alien space; a bit of your house is coming along with you. Soon, instead of sitting at home and thinking about abroad, you'll be scrunched on a plane pretending you're in your den. Kindle doesn't have quite the same power, and it deprives you of the satisfaction of lightening your load as you go. But it's great if you like traveling with a small library.

Brushing my teeth, I take in my bathroom: the posters, the paintings (souvenirs of trips), the shower curtain with its map of the world—my destination a mocking, uninviting dot. Everything I do now has a disconcerting note of potential finality. Of course I'll be back—if all goes well. "To leave is to die a little," the French say (that's what you get for learning French instead of German). Few of us want to die. I climb into bed, that warm embrace, with a sense of security whose time is running out. Awaiting is a succession of unimaginable beds.

The morning of departure I don't want to go anywhere. Leave all this? What was I thinking? Then I arrive at the airport and am knocked to my senses by the lavish, seductive crush of the world.

Movement

For two years in the late eighties, I worked at the *Providence Journal* in Rhode Island and a couple Fridays a month I would walk to the station to board the train for Philadelphia, where Hania was working. While waiting for the train to arrive, I would read the words of Robert Louis Stevenson inscribed in the station floor: FOR MY PART, I TRAVEL NOT TO GO ANYWHERE, BUT TO GO. I TRAVEL FOR TRAVEL'S SAKE. THE GREAT AFFAIR IS TO MOVE.

No statement could have been less appropriate for the people waiting for Amtrak. We were all traveling to go somewhere—New Haven, New York, home—and the great affair was to get there. None of us was a traveler in the spirit of Stevenson. Yet, I always took pleasure in reading his message. It was not just the words and the sentiment, but the fact that they were set down in marble. It was the institutional recognition of a romantic ideal.

I rode the train because I didn't have a car. My Datsun had been totaled while I had been living in Philadelphia and I hadn't worked up the energy to shop for a new one. Also, for short distances at least, I liked to walk.

Commuting to work on foot, I was far from a vagabond, but I was still employing the simplest and oldest mode of transportation.

There was a certain satisfaction in walking out the door in the morning and not climbing into a car or waiting for a bus (dependent on engines, machinery, gas), but primitively continuing to put one leg out in front of the other. For years, my favorite travel book title had been Laurie Lee's *As I Walked Out One Midsummer Morning*—with all its sunny, alliterative promise—and the travel book I held above all others was Patrick Leigh Fermor's two-volume masterpiece about his walk in the 1930s from the Hook of Holland to Constantinople, *A Time of Gifts* and *Between the Woods and the Water*. Not that, strolling through downtown Providence, I imagined myself on the Great Hungarian Plain.

However, heading to the morning editorial meeting I would sometimes think back to a more interesting walk—one I had done from Warsaw to Częstochowa in 1982. That summer, I was coming to the end of my stay in Poland after two years of living in the capital. I decided that a fitting finale would be to march through the countryside on the August pilgrimage to the shrine of the Black Madonna. In the month preceding, I walked all over Warsaw—taking my cue from another beloved book: Alfred Kazin's *A Walker in the City*—and when I got tired I headed to the library and read Władysław Reymont's account of the pilgrimage in 1894 (thirty years before he won the Nobel Prize in Literature).

On the morning of departure, I walked with thousands of Poles as thousands more lined the streets to wish us Godspeed. Workers sat atop factory walls, flashing the V sign; frail widows gazed at us with tear-filled eyes. Martial law was still in effect, following the crackdown on Solidarity the previous December, and large gatherings were illegal, a situation that—coupled with the Church's unflinching stand against communism—turned the annual religious rite into a flowing political rally. The slow pace gave us the time to soak in the scene, the emotion of which took our minds off the effort. I hardly realized that I was walking, and dearly wished the entire 150-mile route could be so spirited.

Over the next nine days I learned a lot about Poland—each group had its own microphones for sermons, lectures, hymns, prayers—and discovered the highs and lows of long-distance walking. There was the mind-numbing monotony of one step endlessly followed by another (though the cast of characters helped relieve the boredom) and the immense, almost martial satisfaction of entering a town or village on foot (heightened by the reception from the residents, some of whom turned out in traditional dress).

I also felt in touch with the country—following its paths, crossing its fields, kicking up its dust—in a way I never had in Warsaw. I came to understand what, years later, Geoff Nicholson would explain in *The Lost Art of Walking*: that walking through a place, like writing about a place, is a way to possess it.

Large numbers of people have discovered this in the north of Spain, on *El Camino de Santiago* (while northern Europeans who spend entire winters in the south rarely feel such a connection to Andalusia). Paulo Coelho's novel *The Pilgrimage*, published in 1987, is usually credited with (or blamed for) the popularization of the pilgrimage to Santiago de Compostela, which has become a modern-day phenomenon, attracting an international crowd and inspiring an endless flow of books. The mix of physical discomfort and spiritual quest, blisters and redemption (in the country of Don Quixote!), has proven irresistible to publishers. Yet even pilgrims who don't write about their journeys discover the novelty of using their legs for travel.

Walking to get someplace has not only a simplicity—no car to pack, no train to catch—but also an authenticity. Like the ancients, you hoist your possessions on your back, your world in a sack, and you set off down the road. You may not speak the language, but as a walker you often don't have to, as there are no scowling ticket sellers to deal with, no confusing schedules to decipher. At some point you'll probably need directions, but then you'll be standing face-to-face, in the open air, with someone who may be a fellow walker.

The thrill of walking comes not so much from movement—except for the initial turning of a step out the door into a journey—but from its gifts of freedom and nonconformity. In a world built on speed, walking somewhere is an act of rebellion. You reject every type of contraption that your forebears have invented to get you there faster—including the bicycle—for your own two legs. You head out into the world while turning your back on its ways.

You do this because, even with a destination in mind, you are interested primarily in the journey. In this way you're very Stevensonian: it's not about where you go, but how. You see fewer landscapes than the passengers on the train do (at least those not lost in electronic pastimes), but the ones you pass through you observe in great detail. And you do more than pass through them; you become a part of them. Like the trees, you are exposed to the sun, the wind, the rain, the mud, which is where the feeling of possession begins: The once foreign land is now all over your boots.

I walked the Kiso Road, with a friend, in November of 2009. It is a fifty-one-mile stretch of the old Nakasendō, which once connected Edo (Tokyo) with Kyoto. I had been to Japan once, visiting those two cities and a few others (and traveling, of course, by train to all of them). I don't speak the language and, unlike many people, I don't feel a strong attraction to the culture. But walking over mist-covered mountains, smelling pine needles in pristine forests, hearing the gurgle of water in village troughs, biting into apples presented by ancient caretakers in lonely temples, inhaling for nine days the damp autumnal air—not to mention sleeping on cold floors in unheated inns—I felt as close to Japan as a mute tourist can.

The trick for walkers is to feel blessed but not superior. After all, it took a plane and a train to get us to the start of the Kiso Road, where—for the first few days—we were buzzed by cars along Route 19.

A few months after I became the travel editor of the *South Florida Sun-Sentinel* in 1989, I received a story from a local man who had recently driven the *camino* in Spain. He was a devout Catholic (unlike most of today's pilgrims), retired and frail, so walking was not an option. I published his story, after some editing, convinced that no readers would object to an American taking a car to Santiago.

None did. As the country of the automobile, we are also the country of the road trip (which, clearly, is exportable). Getting behind the wheel and heading down the highway is an inalienable right, the way that many of us pursue our happiness. The astute immigrant Vladimir Nabokov understood this when he put Humbert Humbert and Lolita in a car and sent them off across the US.

The road trip has long been an American ideal, and its apotheosis is the one that goes coast to coast. We come in two types: those who've driven cross-country and those who dream of doing so. As inspiration we have our literature: John Steinbeck's *Travels with Charley*, Jack Kerouac's *On the Road*, Henry Miller's *The Air-Conditioned Nightmare*, William Least Heat-Moon's *Blue Highways*. Each in his writerly way was in search of America, but only Kerouac approached it (in a style as spontaneous as Nabokov's was fastidious) by making the driving his principal subject, using it as a metaphor for the country: the youthful enthusiasm, the nameless yearning, the glorious promise, and, often unmentioned, the fantastic privilege— gifted dropouts tooling around half a continent as if it were their strange, resplendent backyard. Kerouac's treatment was described as novelistic, though it has been discovered that Steinbeck made up a good number of the encounters that he wrote about. As someone who finds *Travels with Charley* depressingly short on dialogue, I almost wish he had fabricated more.

While never really in decline, the road trip experienced a rebirth after 9/11. Planes were suddenly suspect, and getting onto them had become an ordeal. Climbing into the car, we didn't need to show a photo ID or take off our shoes. Once on the road, there was no danger from terrorists (just other drivers). We could go thousands of miles without ever needing a passport.

I never truly appreciated the giddy sensation of unfettered driving until I took Hania to South Dakota. It was her first trip to the Great Plains and she sat rapt in the passenger seat as we drove down a road that dipped in front of us and an empty, infinitesimally thinning line extended into a featureless, seemingly endless space. Then we switched places. The act of driving—putting her foot on the gas (to the floor if she had wanted), not needing to steer—had an almost intoxicating effect on her. No longer a passenger, she could actually feel and experience the immense, humbling, alien emptiness.

I've gone cross-country twice on land, but never by car. (One of these days, Hania, one of these days.) The first trip was on Greyhound, from Philadelphia to Los Angeles. The fare was $99 one way, the same as on the then new airline People Express, which would have cut my travel time by about sixty-five hours. But I wanted to see the country I was finally crossing (after living and traveling around Europe).

Well I did. And I was happy that I did. But I was happy to fly home on People Express.

About ten years later, I returned to Los Angeles on a train I had boarded in Miami.

Trains are infinitely preferable to buses. There are train buffs; there are no bus buffs. A bus is simply a way to get from one place to another cheaply. A train frequently serves as mere transportation—as it did for me when I was living in Providence—but it is often, itself, a reason to travel.

A train, as Paul Theroux has masterfully shown, is a salon—a moving confessional. Tony Judt called it "a creator of sociability." You can talk to people on buses, but they're not always the people you really want to be talking to; and if you're cornered, you're trapped. On a train, you can always express a need to stretch your legs or grab a sandwich.

Even when they're carrying commuters, trains can give birth to interesting conversations. I dubbed the train I took to Philadelphia

"The Ivy League Local" because, starting in Boston, it made stops near six of the eight prestigious campuses: Harvard, Brown, Yale, Columbia, Princeton, and Penn. Students, not surprisingly, made up a large percentage of the passengers and, while some were obviously going for the Dean's List, others welcomed a chance to put down their yellow highlighters. This was in the days before the much more controlling and antisocial laptop.

In the winter of 1979, I took a series of trains that I called "The Iron Curtain Local." My Polish visa had expired—I had refused the invitation to become an informer that would have extended it indefinitely—so one cold February evening in Warsaw I kissed Hania goodbye and boarded the night train to Budapest. After walking the surprisingly bright streets of Pest, I got the night train to Bucharest (a newfound bleakness), from which I fled on another night train to Sofia. (My final destination was Athens, where I had a friend I was counting on to help me find a job.) For five days I ate very little; I slept sitting up (no available couchettes) and never for very long. In the middle of the night, invariably, the compartment door would bolt open, the lights would come ablaze, and stern men in uniforms would bark commands. The train had reached another border. Half-dreaming passengers would fumble for their passports, all of which were examined and quickly returned with the exception of mine, which was always taken away for closer inspection. For what seemed like hours, I sat in the glare of suspicious, resentful strangers. I was the impediment to our continued movement.

It was an unpleasant experience, just what many travel writers seek. Along with material, it provided a memory that made me less likely to complain when sitting in a dining car stuck in the middle of Texas. The laggardness of trains—which Amtrak has refined through frequent breakdowns and mysterious delays—guarantees that a large number of passengers, especially on the long-distance routes, are people who are not in any rush to get anywhere. The fairly high fares rule out the homeless and the unemployed, which means that you get a lot of retirees, who can be fascinating when they're not discussing their ailments. This probably explains why there are books about the Orient Express, the Trans–Siberian Railway, and the Old Patagonian Express, but none about the Silver Meteor. Although *The Old Patagonian Express* does begin with Theroux taking the Lake Shore Limited and the Lone Star on his way to South America.

But generally, the antiquated nature of trains—in a vast, fast-forward country—makes them a meeting place for kindred spirits: people who not only have time, but wouldn't mind setting it back a few decades. One February, coming home on Amtrak from Mardi Gras in Mobile, I met a woman who was taking her teenage son to see spring training in West Palm Beach. Trains and baseball. I wanted to nominate her for Mother of the Year.

Lovers of trains are escapists who still want to see what it is that they're escaping. Ships and planes both carry you away from the world, then surround you with water and sky, so the isolation is total. Trains remove you from the fray while taking you right through it. (As impressive a trick as flying, really.) They glide through the middle of town and you gaze from your seat, or look up from your breakfast, as schools, mail trucks, and barking dogs pass by. Just inches away, life as you know it continues. You observe it coolly, with the air of someone given a short reprieve. Riding a train is as close as we get to the fantasy of dying and then looking down on the action.

Writers, especially songwriters, have memorialized the movement of trains and the sounds they produce. Although, the modern ones— Japan's bullet trains and France's TGVs—create more of a whoosh than a clickety-clack. Last-in-the-class Amtrak sometimes uses tracks so old that the once hypnotic repetition is replaced by a disturbing, arrhythmic clatter (making classical music one of Amtrak's few contemporary counterparts).

Yet everyone who's ever taken Amtrak knows the intense joy that is felt when—after sitting for half an hour in the middle of a field—

the train slowly, gradually, begins to move forward. When it goes backwards, you head for the bar.

Ships are a twenty-first century paradox: seldom used for transportation—as with amusement rides, you get off where you got on—and yet growing in popularity, number, and size.

PortMiami on a Saturday in winter conjures images of Manhattan in the 1950s, when a headdress of ocean liners feathered its west side. Though in Florida the skies are cleaner, the hulls whiter, the ships boxier, the departures simpler, and the dreams duller.

Cruise ships sail out of sight of land, yet they offer more activities and diversions than most small towns do. They are so packed with entertainment options—rock climbing, ice skating, surfing, shopping—that going on a cruise is as much an immersion as it is an escape.

Enclosed in their floating cities, passengers often overlook the original and most obvious pleasure of ships: the experience of being at sea. Few of them take the time to stand by the railing and look out at the water: a sight that relaxes, impresses, and confounds (as does the passage of 225,000 tons across it). I was on a cruise ship once and, at dusk, found myself the only passenger outside on the promenade deck. After the sun had dropped into the sea and the colors faded from the sky, I went inside and found, by the doors to the dining room, five couples waiting to have their pictures taken before a painted backdrop of a sunset.

Today's cruise ships differ immeasurably from the old ocean liners. In 1975 I took the *QE2* to France, where I was going for a year to study French and, I hoped, get the experience I needed to become a travel writer. A ship seemed the proper mode of transportation for such a critical act. The onboard life of afternoon tea and evenings in the disco was sharpened not just by its brevity—five days from New York to Le Havre—but by the surrounding nothingness. The contrast became even more pronounced at night, when our lights blazed merrily in the middle of a fearsome, watery darkness.

The crossing was so exceptional that, for my return, I booked passage on the *Mikhail Lermontov*. Also, I didn't like the idea of being back home in a mere eight hours, especially after my successful *wanderjahr* (I had not only learned French, I'd worked on a farm). Extended sojourns, the *QE2* had taught me, demand leisurely transits. I wanted time to think about things, and the middle of the ocean was the perfect place to do it.

I made my third and probably last crossing six years later when, still a little weary from the pilgrimage, I left Poland on the *Stefan Batory*. (Hania would join me in a few months.) As the ship inched away from the dock in Gdynia, a band on the pier played *Pożegnanie Ojczyzny* ("Farewell to the Fatherland"), a haunting and all-too-familiar polonaise. None of my previous departures had been so beautifully graced.

The music was fitting, for the ship carried a good number of immigrants. The ocean liners—especially the Polish and Russian ones—had fewer amenities than today's cruise ships (the Russian crew worked in the evenings as entertainers) but a richer mix of passengers. Along with the immigrants you found students, retirees, Peace Corps volunteers, diplomats changing posts, Soviet sympathizers promoting peace (at least on the *Lermontov*), and the inevitable German backpackers heading off to (or back from) South America.

People who board cruise ships are beginning their vacations; those who filled the old ocean liners were very often starting new chapters in their lives. But sailing on a cruise ship does share something with traveling on an ocean liner, and that is the complete sensory experience. Passengers not only see and feel and hear but—thanks to the salt air—taste and smell their passage through the world. That is, if they step outside.

Airplanes constitute another paradox of travel: most used, least loved. No family ever put an airport under its Christmas tree. You don't get ceremonial send-offs when you take a plane (though in China in the nineties the ground crews would often stand and wave).

Nor can you visit the one that changed your life—as I did every time the *QE2* sailed into Port Everglades, three miles from my condo, before its ignominious move to Dubai.

The introduction to Clive James's *Flying Visits*, published in 1984, is a rare and heartfelt hymn to planes. James grew up near the airport in Sydney and learned to identify every nonliving thing in his childhood skies. Since that time, airline passengers have gone from a minority of the fearful to a majority of the disgruntled. Everyone who has flown is distressingly familiar with the injustices. But if you've ever doubted the pleasure that movement can give, note your reaction the next time you're sitting at your gate for twenty minutes, looking at your watch and thinking about your connection, and finally, almost imperceptibly, your plane nudges backwards. It is as uplifting as takeoff (and a lot less stressful).

Once airborne, you enter a peaceful if tightly-bunched limbo— suspended, literally, between earth and heaven, past and future, the deadlines of departure and the chaos of arrival. Unless you're traveling with children, you're removed from all responsibilities. You can read a novel, watch a movie, listen to music without interruption. Where else do you have this luxury? Some people open their laptops and work, oblivious to the blessings of unstructured time, a meaningless lull, and, outside the window, a shifting neighborhood of eye-level clouds.

We tell people of our frights on planes—dinner trays flying, passengers praying—but rarely of our idylls: not because we don't have them or because, like Tolstoy's happy families, they're all alike, but because they're more personal.

Once on a flight from Fort Lauderdale to San Francisco, fiddling with the buttons on my armrest, I came across the confiding, long-lost voice of Gordon Lightfoot. In my youth I'd been a big fan. He was not singing "If You Could Read My Mind," which you can sometimes hear on oldies stations, but "Approaching Lavender," which I hadn't listened to in over two decades.

He was followed by more old friends not heard from in years, at least not with these songs: Joni Mitchell singing "Ladies of the Canyon," James Taylor doing "Carolina In My Mind" (a perfect traveling song, even if you're going to California). I had boarded a plane that, unbeknownst to me, had obtained the soundtrack of my college years.

Spiking the nostalgia was serendipity (which you can't get from an iPod). I thought back to August of '73, flying home from my summer in London and listening, as the plane ascended, to Ralph Vaughan Williams's "English Folk Song Suite." The music was new to me, so it became forever wedded in my mind to the exhilaration of takeoff and the sweet anticipation of homecoming. It gave me the first of many shining in-flight moments.

They tend to occur most frequently on long overseas flights, often during dinnertime. There is something about the lightheadedness produced by free food, piped-in music, fussing flight attendants, and wee bottles of wine at thirty thousand feet that makes you susceptible. Especially when added to the relief of finally being in the air. In an hour you'll be missing your bed, but right now you're raising your glass. Sunlight streams through an unshaded window like an affirmation.

Somewhere over the Midwest, Ralph McTell came on. I drove my college roommates crazy listening to "Streets of London" over and over—"How can you tell me, you're lo-one-ly"—only now there was no one else around to hear it. It was like a balm that I had deprived myself of for years.

It wasn't the last. The airline, catering to my youthful tastes in music with an accuracy that was almost alarming, had added "The Ferryman," another moving ballad.

"Oh the traveler he is weary, the traveling man he is tired."

It could have been describing any number of people in my vicinity. Me, I felt light as a cloud.

Break from Routine

In the world of travel, planes, ships, and trains all hold dominion over cars because they relieve their passengers of the responsibility of control. As relaxing as many Americans find driving, it's still confining, both physically—you're not only seated, you're strapped into the seat—and behaviorally: you can't, or shouldn't, drink a beer, send a text, take a nap.

But the real advantage of the three is that they're not your normal means of getting around. You can drive to Patagonia but you'll still be doing what you do every day. You change your sky but not your habits, to paraphrase Horace. While taking a train, even to the next state, would constitute an invigorating change of pace for many Americans.

The reason I couldn't sleep before a class trip to the Hackettstown Fish Hatchery had nothing to do with fish. It was tied to the fantastic notion that in the morning, while my brothers would be sitting at their desks listening to their teachers, I would be on a bus looking out the window. I would be out in the world on a school day.

In large part, the attraction of travel is that it's not everyday life. You look down at the Grand Canyon from thirty thousand feet and, added to the beauty of the view, is the thought of your colleagues back at the office. Wanderlust meets schadenfreude.

It's true that many of the people back at the office are there by choice. They've earned time off but they don't take it; they are that strange group of people who shirk vacation.

The practice became more prevalent as the economy worsened. People who would genuinely have liked to get away, to experience a change of scenery, feared the consequences of being out of the office for a week. So they stayed on the job, along with the workaholics, the narcissists, and the control freaks who help make the idea of vacation so appealing.

New surroundings are free of the imperfections of the old ones. They have their own faults (though travel magazine photographs try to prove otherwise), but they're not faults you're condemned to live with. Your tour guide may be bossy, but he's not your boss.

We tend to think of vacation as a break from work more than from routine—a much-needed rest after fifty weeks of toil. This idea, along with the recession, was the force behind the staycation (a word that is almost as distasteful for me to type as it is to utter). Just relax at home, or spend a few nights at a nearby hotel: sleep in, eat out, forget about the guy who monopolizes meetings.

The problem with this is that, though you're not getting up and going to work, you're still at home or at least in your hometown. Your days are less hectic but your surroundings are the same. You are deprived of the power of temporary change.

Change, even short-lived, is too much for some people. Creatures of habit find the disruptions of travel unbearable. "I wouldn't mind seeing China," Philip Larkin said, "if I could come back the same day." Type A personalities abhor the waiting, the frequent idleness. "I had done enough traveling," Paul Theroux wrote in *Granta* in 1989, "to know that half of it was delay or nuisance." Perfectionists can't bear the unpredictability, the randomness, the improvisation. Know-it-alls don't do well when they can't speak the language.

When any of these people travel, they tend to overprepare, overplan, and overpack.

The American mother and daughter I met in Turkey gave me a lift in their rental car in Cappadocia. While the daughter drove, the mother passed me a bag of Pepperidge Farm Milanos. I happily ate one, all the while wondering what would possess someone to bring sweets to the country of Turkish delight. Isn't one of the pleasures of traveling trying new foods? I'm sure they did—they had prepared for the trip by watching Turkish films—but just in case, they had in reserve a stash of American processed treats. They changed their sky but not their snacks.

Perhaps the Milanos were their way of acknowledging that, however far we travel, we cannot change who we are; we cannot change our souls. Still, munching on them felt to me like cheating.

This is how many people confront change—by bringing along something dear. It is more admirable than staying at home. And many Americans do stay home—only about a third of us possess passports—usually out of incuriosity, sometimes intimidation (which terrorism is now contributing to).

There is an uncertainty about travel that affects even seasoned travelers. For us it's mostly exciting, but there's always a feeling of anxiety in abandoning (even for a short time) what we know (even if it's tedium). To travel is to make yourself vulnerable—leaving, with your papers and plastic, the high-tech security of your home and wandering sumptuously among imperfect strangers. Couples by definition take the familiar with them; for solo travelers, the apprehension is greater—and women have their own concerns.

A break from routine is a joy that can also be a hurdle. We are conditioned to love the comfort of habit; otherwise, how would we ever get any work done? John Updike, the poet laureate of everyday life, said in an interview once that he never embraced the writings of Kerouac because of a Protestant (my word, not his) belief that we couldn't all go off on the road. Some of us had to stay home, make a living, and raise a family.

Yet as Updike showed in *Bech: A Book* (in which a Jewish novelist goes on an author tour behind the Iron Curtain), everyone needs a break now and then. Even those who find change difficult, reap its rewards. What doesn't totally freak you out makes you more interesting, tolerant, and sweet. Also, it gives you something to talk about.

For decades, writers, especially British ones, used travel as a break from routine. Charles Dickens, Anthony Trollope, D. H. Lawrence, Aldous Huxley, Graham Greene, and Evelyn Waugh all took time off from novels to write travel books: a tradition that added immeasurably to English literature (though not, sadly, the syllabi of English departments). Just as regrettably, only V. S. Naipaul and, more lucratively, Paul Theroux have continued the practice. These writers' journeys got them out of the house and their heads, while giving them—at least in the case of the last four—subjects for their fiction.

Greene, one of the most peripatetic writers of the twentieth century, titled his second memoir *Ways of Escape*. His life was a constant battle against boredom, which explains his restlessness. Travel allows you to change, even if briefly, your scenery, schedule, diet, perspective, etc. Away from home, you're no longer repeating set behaviors. The shock of the unfamiliar clears your mind of the dull. A simple, physical travel pleasure for me is eating foods (fried chicken with biscuits and gravy comes to mind) that I wouldn't allow my health-conscious self at home but become (or so I tell myself) an essential part of my experience of the place. Then someone I meet tells me that Southern food never tastes better than when eaten at a funeral, and I start to contemplate the connection between the culinary and funerary arts.

Travel can provide a kind of make-believe life overhaul (or a real one if you decide to prolong your stay). It allows you to slip out of yourself and try on a second language, a famous city, a new persona, and see how they feel. It is a vacation from so much more than work.

The year I spent in France I started in Provence, at a language school for foreign students. Rather than a transformation, I experienced a regression: one year out of college and I was back living in a dorm, eating in a student cafeteria, and walking to morning classes (though this time on cobblestones past moss-covered fountains).

When the school year ended I traveled to Alsace, where I found a job on a farm. The student I had been for most of my life became a farmhand. The compatriots and other foreigners who had surrounded me in Provence were replaced by a three-generational Alsatian family that fed me, clothed me, and treated me like a beloved cousin. They also gave me daily lessons in French, agriculture, history, music. (Dany, who was my age, loved to sing, and had a repertoire that ranged from Bizet to Brassens to bawdy medical school ditties.) I had changed much more than my sky; my chores, habits, meals, and even my speech were different now. Leading the cows out to pasture, or making a joke at the dinner table, I would sometimes pull back and marvel quietly at who I had become (at least for a summer). I had moved so far, and in such an unexpected direction, from my previous life that I felt an almost disbelieving happiness.

After I left the farm, I discovered that the experience was indelible. Now, whenever I speak French—even in Florida, though especially when I return to France—I become a slightly different person. I step out of my everyday self. A friend of mine in California—who lived, worked, and married in Japan—claims that whenever he speaks Japanese, he becomes Japanese (to such an extent that he will bow to the person he's talking to on the phone).

A few years later in Poland, I again experienced dumbstruck delight at my unlikely fate. I was teaching at Warsaw's only private school for English. The English Language College was a revered institution in the center of the city that filled in the evenings with teachers who spoke the King's English (often without ever having left Poland) and young, intelligent, dedicated students. Both groups gave a nightly lie to Americans' ignorant perceptions of Poles.

Teaching was less of a stretch for me, as a profession, than farming. Here it was more the setting than my job that amazed me, for I had inexplicably found myself a place—an engaged, intense, fascinating life—in the lusterless capital of a communist country in a cut-off, marginal part of Europe. The fact that Warsaw was a city that most Americans would not care to visit, let alone live in, made more exquisite my sense of belonging.

Of course, working there I had traded, as in Alsace, one routine for another. However, with Solidarity, strikes, and threats of Soviet tanks, Poland was anything but routine in those years. The feeling of uncertainty was constant; even the Poles found themselves in new terrain.

The day-to-day in another country can be drastically different, at least for the non-immigrant, from daily life back home. Abroad, you're always learning and constantly caught off guard. Each new dawn promises, if not an adventure, a potential embarrassment. This is why narcissists tend to stay at the office.

They shouldn't. There is a place out there even for people wedded to routine. In fact, taking your ingrained habits with you can produce wildly and wonderfully unpredictable results.

I'm an Episcopalian, so I sometimes go to church when I travel. It's a good way to meet the locals (and, in some countries, the expats). You're less likely to get a cold shoulder at the coffee hour than you are at a bar. At church, no one thinks you're hitting on them.

One Sunday morning in Bangkok, I took a taxi to Christ Church and saw a city that no tourists see. (Who flies to Bangkok and goes to church?) In Mumbai, I went to Holy Communion at St. Thomas Cathedral, and afterwards talked to one of the choir members, who told me she was a Roman Catholic. Suneta invited me to *her* church, the Cathedral of the Holy Name, which had Masses every day.

When I arrived on the appointed day, Suneta—who was active in cathedral life here as well—insisted that I read the lesson. I felt more flustered than honored. First, I reminded her, I wasn't Catholic. And, as would be clear to everyone in the congregation, I wasn't Indian. As a travel writer, I love participating in the life of a place, but usually in private—getting invited home for dinner—where my outsider status is not broadcast. Then I can feel like an explorer, at worst an intruder. Reading the lesson, I would feel like an imposter.

It tells you something about Suneta's skills of persuasion that, twenty minutes later, I stood at the lectern and read the day's lesson. There were no audible gasps from the pews; in fact, after the service one gentleman complimented me on my reading. (He said he appreciated it when readers established occasional eye contact with their audience.) Yet, afterwards, I kept thinking of the strangeness of it all: an American Episcopalian reading the lesson in the Catholic cathedral in the heart of Mumbai. In four decades of travel, it is one of the oddest things I've done—and it grew out of a normal Sunday activity.

You don't have to travel far, though, to experience the beauty of a break from routine. The inevitability of this joy, as with movement and anticipation, makes the destination irrelevant. (The whys of travel always trump the wheres.) You can visit the next county and you'll still be removed from the repetitions of home. You may feel aimless, but you won't be doing things by rote.

Not long after we moved to Fort Lauderdale, Hania and I drove west on Alligator Alley to spend a weekend on Sanibel Island. We stayed in a modest cottage motel, ate our morning pancakes at the local breakfast spot (its walls covered with pictures of lighthouses), and, naturally, searched for shells. We both remarked on how the place felt like the seashore in a way that Fort Lauderdale never did.

Our hometown is more built-up than Sanibel, a medium-sized city compared to a sparsely populated island, but it's still the seashore for the thousands of vacationers who come to its beaches every year. It was not just Sanibel but what we were doing there—or, more important, not doing—that made it seem like a sandy idyll. We were not working, paying bills, running errands, seeing friends—all the things we do at home. Instead we lounged around, slowed our pace, and drank in the place. We could do this sometime in Fort Lauderdale, but it would mean taking an onerous staycation.

~

One of the reasons I don't like tours is that they replace one routine with another. You follow a schedule (goodbye serendipity) and you go with a group (farewell chance encounters). That first day at breakfast the faces are different from the ones you normally see there, but they're the ones you'll be seeing there every morning of your trip. Having already paid, you're not necessarily willing to bolt.

In 2001, I went on a tour to Cuba. It was the only way tourists could see the island legally, providing the tour had an "educational" purpose. Because of this stipulation, a part of most days included a government visit; almost every morning, it seemed, we were driven to some new office or center for the obligatory spiel about international friendship. I was there as a travel editor—an insignificant position in any newsroom—and ended up attending more meetings in Havana than I did in a month in Fort Lauderdale. Not to mention, I sat through every one of them with all the people I had seen at breakfast.

Like all tours, this one constituted a compromised form of travel. Real travel doesn't swap routines; it feeds you a steady diet of the irregular and the unforeseen. It may not—it *will* not—all be pleasant ("delay or nuisance," if you're lucky), but the unpleasantness is bearable because it's not subject to regular life's law of momentum. If you get laid off on Monday, chances are your week will be grim. But if you have a bad night in Berlin, there's nothing keeping you from having a great next night in Prague. Only the traveler goes to sleep with absolutely no idea what tomorrow will bring.

In the summer of 2001, I took a night train from St. Petersburg to Vilnius. I had had an interesting time in Russia, but I was happy to be leaving. There was a kind of lawlessness in the new freedom, which itself was incomplete. I had needed a visa, and to get it I had to indicate where I'd be sleeping every night of my visit. (It was in the cramped study of a cheerless apartment rented by a strictly entrepreneurial couple, as all the hotels were booked for the White Nights.)

The day of my departure, a massive traffic jam—the first I had seen—killed any chances of getting a taxi to the station. Disobeying all the tourist warnings, I hailed a private car. It was more sedate than my train, where, sometime after midnight, I awoke to find a man sitting on my bed, another man sitting on the one opposite, and a makeshift table between them holding their vodka bottles and playing cards. They had noticed, I assumed, my nearly empty compartment and thought it a good place to continue their game.

I got up and grumbled a complaint, though of course *I* was the one disrespectful of the national indifference to privacy. I grabbed my things and headed off in search of another compartment.

The train pulled into Vilnius shortly after dawn. I wheeled my bag down cobblestone streets. I asked directions of a stylish young woman with thick blond hair who didn't speak English. (I had no Lithuanian, so we communicated in Polish.) I entered the Old Town, recently woken up from a half century of communism, and found a stately house that had been turned into a hotel. Business was slow (the place had just opened), prices were good, and there was a room with a view. Plopping on the bed, I turned on the TV and read the words: WELCOME, MR. SWICK. Still in the former Soviet Union, I had unmistakably returned to the West.

A more fateful change-of-fortune experience occurred after I had left the farm in Alsace. On my way to England to get the *Mikhail Lermontov*, I stopped in Brussels to see a woman I had met my first week in Provence. Anne had quickly headed home from France, deciding she could work on her French in her own Francophone country. Over the previous months, we had exchanged a few letters.

I found a cheap hotel and went to her house (or rather that of her parents, with whom she was living). She seemed a different woman; I didn't remember her as mousy and depressive. The house was gloomy, too: filled with heavy furniture and the smell of cooking grease. I told her I'd meet her tomorrow after work.

The next morning, I walked out of the hotel and boarded the train to Ostend. (I had paid for the first night on my arrival.) I felt like a cad, even though there was nothing between us save a few letters. But I was acting on more than a desire, almost a need, to leave. As if the impulse driving me went beyond that of mere escape.

That evening, on the ferry to England, I stuck my hand in my jacket pocket and felt my room key. In my haste to make my getaway, I had forgotten to return it. The discovery increased my sense of guilt; there were now two entities in Brussels I had left in the lurch. The only thing that comforted me slightly was the fact that I was a traveler, someone just passing through—and pass through I had. This idea would make, I hoped, any disappointment or inconvenience I had caused a bit more acceptable. If it didn't (looking at things selfishly again), I wouldn't be around to know about it. A break from routine is also, often, a break from responsibility.

I removed the key from my pocket. It was a large key, with an attachment, the sort that used to hang on hooks or reside in small cubicles behind reception desks. I walked with it to the ship's railing, tossed it high into the air, and watched it fall into the English Channel.

I was probably inspired by a passage in Evelyn Waugh's *When the Going Was Good*, which I had bought in Paris on my way to Provence (one of the few books in English I allowed myself that year). Toward the end of "A Pleasure Cruise in 1929," Waugh described himself, on the last night, walking outside and throwing his champagne glass over the side. It was a spontaneous gesture that became, he wrote, "bound up with the turgid, indefinite feelings of homecoming."

My key toss was more of a portent. In a few days, in another hotel, I would meet a young woman named Hania.

Novelty

The biggest lie in travel—greater than "For you my friend, a special deal"—is "Every place now looks the same." You hear it all the time, uttered by people who would never say something as lame and clichéd (and along the same lines) as, "There's nothing new under the sun." The second statement brands you as old, out-of-touch, incurious, while the first, for some strange reason, suggests a hard-earned world-weariness. Instead of the wrong-headed platitude that it is, it's taken as the callous wisdom of the seasoned traveler.

It's also a kind of one-upmanship (for such a personal activity, travel can be surprisingly competitive), a way of distinguishing one's past journeys (and self) from today's packaged tours (and tourists). It's a variation on "Capri (or Tangier or Goa or wherever) isn't what it used to be." Already in the 1930s, D. H. Lawrence was complaining, on a visit to New Mexico: "There is no mystery left. We've been there, we've seen it, we know all about it. We've done the globe and the globe is done."

For some people, these statements lend the speaker an aura of authority, authenticity, and privileged knowledge: He (it's usually the males who boast) was there when. For the more discerning, they reveal him as a jaded bore.

I live in a part of Florida—the southeast coast—where most of the cities are built according to an identical blueprint: an east-west main street and a bridge to a barrier island. They all share the same ocean and possess the same vegetation. Yet Miami looks completely different from Fort Lauderdale (especially when you get off the highway), and Hollywood would never be mistaken for Delray Beach. Boca Raton is a world unto itself.

These cities differ even more in character than in physical appearance. Miami is urban and Latin; Fort Lauderdale is suburban and part of the so-called 'sixth borough.' Hollywood is ethnic and bohemian (for Florida at least) while Delray is upscale and well-groomed. A blind woman could tell which city she's in by the sounds on the street.

I realize that when people say "Every place now looks the same" they don't mean it literally. Though, even as a general gripe, it's unfounded and uncalled for. It's more a sign of parochialism than of sophistication; the person who complains about McDonald's everywhere is someone with an unhealthy fixation on chains. It's inaccurate, misleading, and the geographical equivalent—in lazy observation and revealed prejudice—of saying the members of a race all look alike.

One summer morning Hania and I set off on a Florida road trip and stopped around noon in Vero Beach. A few years earlier I had gone there to write about the town (downtown, bridge, island), and met a cattle rancher (ranches enriched the equation) who had built a studio next to his house where he spent his free time painting. The day of my visit Sean was putting the finishing touches on a work based on "The Ambassadors" by Hans Holbein the Younger.

This time, we met him at a restaurant just off I-95. It had nothing in common with the fast-food franchises one usually finds at highway exits; it was a family-run place with catfish, okra, and collard greens on the menu, and old black-and-white photographs of ranchers on the walls. Most of the diners were ranchers like Sean: dressed in work boots, jeans, long-sleeved shirts dark with sweat, and cowboy hats. I sat in my shorts and sandals and marveled—just as I had the day I'd found Sean painting—at the exotic scenery a mere hundred miles north of my home.

It was culture shock four counties up. You don't hear that term very much anymore; it's been replaced by globalization, Americanization, the shrinking planet. We've become so fixated on the world's similarities that we've lost touch with—or simply pretend not to see—its differences.

I'm not sure why. Maybe, secretly, we enjoy finding the familiar; it gives us something to cling to amidst the alien. Perhaps, in the case of American brands, it feeds a latent feeling of patriotism. Jan Morris, one of history's most dedicated and tolerant travelers, never complained about McDonald's; she realized that its proliferation was due to its ability to satisfy a desire. The Big Mac, she explained, belongs to the world. Her generous attitude almost made me want to buy one. Although, I'll admit, on hot summer days in foreign capitals I have sometimes stepped into the bright canteens—invariably more modern and chic than their counterparts in the States—simply to get a drink with ice in it.

Jonathan Raban, leaving Missoula in *Driving Home: An American Journey*, writes of the "fast-food pagodas" and shows how a brilliant writer can take the familiar and make it new. Pico Iyer, on his first trip to China, realized that he had nothing to add to the thousands of words that had been written about the Great Wall. Instead, he found his material—his inspiration—hanging out at the Kentucky Fried Chicken on Tiananmen Square. It was the old travel writer's practice of avoiding the sights and focusing on the people, but with a modern, international business twist.

Iyer in his books, especially his first, *Video Night in Kathmandu*, constantly shows how what we think we know takes on new meaning abroad; and how what we export gets modified or transformed to meet the needs and tastes of the local population. Walk into a 7-Eleven in

Tokyo and you know you're not in Cincinnati. Iyer's books, while often themed to globalization (a later one is titled *The Global Soul*), celebrate the rich and mostly unthreatened variety of the world.

Our planet's diversity begins with the physical. In *The Pillars of Hercules*, an account of a journey around the Mediterranean (a well-traveled place), Paul Theroux wrote: "No one has ever described the place where I have just arrived." It was a pithier version of Anthony Trollope's observation (*Australia and New Zealand*) in 1873: "I doubt whether I have ever read any description of scenery which gave me an idea of the place described." Neither man was taking potshots at his fellow writers; they were both extolling the supremacy of travel.

Today, we have a lot more than words to take us places; there's Instagram, YouTube, and Google Earth, for starters. While virtual travel may diminish the field of travel writers, it won't—or shouldn't—cut into the number of travelers. There is still no substitute for being there.

No technology can replace the visceral experience of arriving in a new place, the moment when you step out of an airport, or off of a ship, and subject yourself—body, mind, and heart—to a strange land. You're attuned to everything: the sights, the sounds, the smells, the textures, and very soon the tastes. I always tell travel writing students to use these early hours to explore, because one's surroundings—the colorful drinks, the melodic sirens, the sweet-and-foul smells—will not be as clear or as sharp in a few days. At the start, everything stands out as if in high definition, especially, strangely, if you're groggy from jet lag or insomnia. (The one time in life when it pays to be tired.) "My nerves," the protagonist in Nabokov's crystalline story "Spring in Fialta" remarks, "were unusually receptive after a sleepless night."

Few things give me as much pleasure as arriving in a new city and walking its streets. My enjoyment varies in intensity, but it's always there, whether I'm in Laramie or Luang Prabang. "Loafing around in a new world," Nicolas Bouvier wrote in *The Way of the World*, "is the most absorbing occupation."

This sentiment explains the appeal of vagabonding over living abroad, which is the travel equivalent of monogamy; its responsibilities and commitments provide a more meaningful, but also more uniform, experience. Travelers who keep moving are rewarded again and again with the new, though, like bachelors, they miss out on the insights and intimacy that result from lengthy stays.

The winter I studied in Provence, I was fairly used to things by Easter, so for the mid-term break I sailed on a ferry from Marseille to Algiers. We left Europe in the evening and the next morning arrived in Africa. Disembarking at the port I experienced, for the first time in my life, the shock of not looking like anyone else. Men—men almost exclusively—passed by with hair, complexions, and sometimes clothes that were emphatically, almost aggressively, different from mine. Standing out—being so obviously not of the place—was a wholly new, disconcerting, intimidating sensation. Today, the most high-tech video camera could capture it all, even the emotions from a close-up of my face, but it couldn't make viewers feel them as I did.

I had a mildly similar experience at the beginning of that year, when I arrived in Paris. My first morning in the city I looked out the window of my hotel, near the Gare de l'Est, and noticed that all of the men on the street were wearing dark trousers. Every one, without exception. I looked for a long time, trying to spot a defector, because I had packed my favorite khakis. Physically, I might be able to pass for a Frenchman (dark hair, slight build) but sartorially, I knew, I would be an obvious, hideous foreigner. The thought gnawed at me like a pain; I seriously hesitated to step outside.

American students who go to Paris today have no such problems; there is now an international style of dressing, especially among the young, that's followed pretty much everywhere. A teenager from Kansas can go to almost any world capital and, clothes-wise at least, fit right in. (Though khakis are still obvious markers of Americans.)

Even with a certain conformity in dress, differences remain. Yes, the world wears jeans, but it doesn't always wear them the way we do:

41

In Paris, it's gauche to wear jeans with sneakers. People who complain that "Every place now looks the same" are not sensitive to subtleties.

When I fly to Paris now, it's familiar but still refreshingly, and sometimes confoundingly, different—especially since I'm arriving from Florida. My reaction is not that I've seen this all before—the odious, obtuse (Lawrentian), "been there, done that"—but that I'm back in a world that is not my own.

Of course, I don't get the same rush that I do when I arrive in a foreign city for the first time. That feeling, the galvanic dive into the maw of the new, is unique, inimitable, occasionally scary, and always intoxicating. It is the force that keeps travelers traveling, like addicts searching for a more intense high.

Arrivals, not surprisingly, provide some of the most enduring memories from our trips.

My first experience with Asia was my trip to Vietnam in 1994. I arrived in Saigon around midnight—from the taxi, I saw a young woman riding side-saddle on the back of a moped—and went straight to sleep in the Rex Hotel. The next morning, I walked out of the lobby and headed toward the river. Once again, I didn't look like any of the people around me, but this fact wasn't as remarkable as it had been in Algiers. (I had gotten somewhat accustomed to the feeling, visiting the Caribbean and avoiding the resorts.) It was a good thing, because it freed me to focus on my surroundings instead of myself.

I eventually came to a wide, tree-lined boulevard where more young women flowed past, this time on bicycles. Many wore the traditional, light-colored tunic (*ao dai*), some holding one hem of it up to the handlebars. A few sported conical hats as protection from the sun; every once in a while one would appear in opera gloves. Through the heat and dust they pedaled serene and spotless, black hair falling like licorice down their backs. The scene, which in a week would become almost passé, fairly shouted: "The East. Vietnam. Saigon. Gotcha."

Cuba intrigued me on a number of levels. It was another world completely (totalitarianly), but one that was less than an hour's plane ride from my home. Havana was a Caribbean metropolis, an oxymoron outside of San Juan and Port-of-Spain. Unlike those two cities, with their beaches and harbors, Havana seemed to have no dividing line between itself and the sea; waves crashed atop the sea wall by our hotel, especially at night, and spread in shallow pools along the street. The city resembled an enormous freighter making its way through stormy waters (and getting nowhere). I enjoyed the unexpectedness of the scene—"No one has ever described the place where I have just arrived"—and the freshness of the metaphor, which I could now use, without attribution.

I had also leafed through a lot of coffee table books on Cuba (as a frequenter of bookstores does in South Florida) and assumed that I had seen, in photographs, pretty much all there was to see in the city. I once went to a town in Spain because of a picture I'd seen in a guidebook of a charming street, and when I got there I discovered that it was a prosaic city except for that one street. I had assumed that the picture was a representation, not an exception. With Havana it was the opposite: I was amazed by how much the photographic albums had left out. The narrow streets and crumbling buildings of Old Havana fed into the wider streets and crumbling buildings of Centro, which in turn led to the broader avenues and crumbling villas of Vedado and Miramar. The profusion and range of architectural richness—from Spanish Colonial to Art Deco to Midcentury Modern—made the decay all the more tragic.

One night in our minivan on our way to a restaurant—two staples from our world that were out of the reach of most Cubans—there was a discussion on how, eventually, McDonald's would move in, and then Starbucks, and Havana would lose its attractiveness. At least to tourists. Sometimes, one person's novelty is another's sad reality. Or, as Dwight Macdonald put it: "The tourist's exotic is the native's poison."

Even when Cuba opens up to foreign investment, and gets its long-awaited and well-deserved taste of Big Macs, the people eating and working at McDonald's will not be like their American counterparts—the same way that the kids wolfing down Royales with Cheese on the Champs-Élysées are a different type of teenager from the ones in Atlanta. They may be wearing baseball caps backwards, and listening to Beyoncé on their iPods, but they don't talk, act, or think like American adolescents. If you took a picture, the scene might look familiar; if you had a conversation, you'd be surprised.

In the past, the most important quality in a traveler was a sense of adventure; today, it is a sense of wonder. We have all become inundated; and the world a little overexposed. Still, for those who travel wide-eyed in an age of information overload, the revelations are more potent (if not more numerous) for being unexpected. And they still await, for no amount of images and data can shatter the preeminence of the personal encounter.

Traveling, we gaze at the historic—which, to our experience, is new and suddenly digestible in all its dimensions—and we stare at the ordinary because to us it's unique. The Parthenon gives us the same giddy shock of the unseen as the octopus hung on the clothesline to dry.

On my high school Latin Clubs trip to Italy we visited Pompeii, of course, and at one point passed a group of European schoolgirls. With great excitement (more among the males than the females I suppose), we noticed they all had hairy legs. The sight exceeded in significance anything we'd seen in the preserved houses (we were not shown the erotic mosaics). Those hirsute calves stayed with me, I always thought, because they had provided a coming-of-age moment in a sheltered, sisterless childhood.

Thirty years later I traveled to China and like most tourists (with the possible exception of Pico Iyer), I went to see the Great Wall. I walked a section of it (impressed by its steepness); I thought of the manpower used to construct it; I tried to picture its prodigious continuation as it disappeared over the hill. I experienced the slight disbelief of finding oneself in the presence of a legendary landmark.

Back on the ground, I went to the men's room. It was a large facility with a long row of stalls. One of the open ones revealed a Chinese man sitting on the toilet and reading a newspaper. The door of the stall was simply a suggestion that he had ignored; everyone knew what he was doing, so why should he hide it from public view? I still see him sitting there quietly, pants at his ankles, clearer today than I see the Great Wall.

Often it's the things we glimpse on our way to the sights that we remember most vividly, because, unlike the must-sees, they catch us off guard. We all know that the Eiffel Tower, the Taj Mahal, and the Alamo are there, which doesn't mean that they don't have the ability to dazzle or disappoint. Yet, it's the streets around them that are the real mystery and, occasionally, revelation. The guidebooks leave out the incidental and the impromptu, which are also the human.

My first day in Warsaw, in 1978, I took a bus to the center and then walked to the Old Town. As I mentioned earlier, there weren't a lot of books about Poland, but I knew about the historic district, which had been leveled during the war and then rebuilt with such attention to detail that, at times, the paintings of Bellotto were consulted. (Bellotto, the nephew of Canaletto, served as the court painter for King Poniatowski.) My route to the Old Town was lined with drab, blocky, post-war buildings, many containing shops with window displays. I became fascinated by the mannequins, which were dressed in outfits as shapeless and colorless as the buildings that housed them. They didn't look like any mannequins I'd ever seen and, in an even stranger disconnect, they didn't resemble any of the women walking on the sidewalk. Young Polish women, even in those days, were very stylish with their boots, scarves, hats, leather bags strung across their chests and resting fetchingly on wool-coated hips. In the first article I wrote from my new home, I noted that it was "the first city I'd seen where the women were more fashionable than the mannequins."

It was an instance of a simple observation—a seeming paradox, a foreigner's puzzlement—revealing something greater. The reason that young women in Warsaw dressed better than the mannequins was that the mannequins never went abroad. Like the rest of the Soviet Bloc, Poland had been saddled with state-owned stores but, unlike its neighbors, it had been granted relaxed travel restrictions. So, many students (like Hania) would spend their summers working in England, or France, or Germany, or Italy (usually the country whose language they were studying) and return in the fall with additions to their wardrobes. Male students, devoted to a uniform of a green army jacket and faded blue jeans, spent their money on other things. After the Old Town, young women were Warsaw's chief visual delight.

However, it's not just through sight that novelty appears; in travel, all our senses are singed by the new. Added to the visual bombardment are masses of unphotographable sounds, smells, flavors, sensations; accents and stenches, prayer calls and sauces, the foreign pillow and the whiskery kiss.

Our enjoyment can also be thwarted by the new. If a break from routine is the joy that, for some people, is also a hurdle, then novelty is the joy that is also a handicap. Sometimes it's simple, short-lived frustration—we eventually figure out how to turn on the lights in our room—but sometimes it's more serious. Tourists have been killed in England because they looked the wrong way before crossing the street.

When I was a travel editor, readers would sometimes call and ask me if certain destinations were safe. These were invariably cities with crime rates much lower than South Florida's. But the callers knew their way around South Florida; they knew where they could, and should not, go, while foreign cities were blank slates to them, filled (they thought) with lurking dangers. Not speaking the language doesn't necessarily build self-confidence either; we become children again (novelty added to novelty), which can be amusing but not so much when you're in need of a restroom, or a train ticket, or a cardiologist. Even when your trip is trouble-free, it's maddening to wander amongst people with whom you can't talk.

Food helps compensate. (Though an inability to speak the language ensures that you miss out on a lot of unadvertised delicacies.) Eating is the easiest and one of the most pleasurable ways to absorb a culture, and it is one of the main reasons many Americans travel. Which makes sense, since travelers helped change the way Americans eat. The craft beer movement, the growth in artisanal bakeries, the trend in specialty chocolates were all, if not started, enthusiastically supported by people, often the young, who returned from Europe significantly altered by what they had tasted. It was impossible to go back to sliced bread after you'd eaten your first baguette; Budweiser lost its appeal to people who had sipped Chimay.

When I was studying in Provence, my parents came for a week, and we rented a car to drive the Côte d'Azur. After our first lunch in St. Tropez, I bought a Toblerone bar to share. My mother—who had grown up not far from Hershey, Pennsylvania—took a bite and an expression of intense pleasure came over her face, touched by a hint of revelation: You mean chocolate can taste like this? It was the moment at which, I think, she began to understand my decision to quit my job and move to France.

Today, Toblerone is sold in my neighborhood supermarket; the local Whole Foods carries Chimay. It's a beautiful thing (unless you're a rabid locavore), as are ethnic restaurants. It would be hard to imagine an American today going to Mexico and tasting his first taco. Most of us eat croissants (often in a highly corrupted form), gazpacho, pad thai, and chicken tikka masala before we ever visit their countries of origin. There's one small disadvantage to this: When we do travel to Spain and eat the cold soup, it's probably different (and no doubt better) than the versions we've had. Yet, it's still familiar—a dish we know, an experience we've been through (albeit in less authentic settings). We're deprived of the gift of initiation. When we return home, we miss out on the transporting power of taste. Risotto Milanese doesn't carry you back to Milan if you first had it in Brooklyn; but if you eat your first snail in Burgundy, every snail afterwards will remind you of Burgundy.

I grew up in a small New Jersey town in the 1950s with parents of German-Irish-Welsh stock (white, Celtic-Saxon Protestants), which means I now rarely go a day without eating a food whose existence I was ignorant of for the first third of my life. Hummus, tapenade, frittata, rapini, arugula, mango immediately come to mind, as well as any cheese not named American, Swiss, cheddar, provolone, or parmesan. The only possible bright side to this cornucopian benightedness is that, as a traveler, I have frequently had my eyes opened by what I've put into my mouth.

In the fall of 1991 I went to Genoa, my first visit to Italy since the Latin Clubs trip. (It looked even better without chaperones.) One morning I stopped at the café next door to my hotel. A thin rectangle of bread sat in a display case; I pointed to it resignedly (I knew Italians weren't big on breakfast), paid, and carried it to a table. Without enthusiasm, I bit into it, and immediately started to salivate. It wasn't stale or dry, as I had expected, but moist with olive oil. Each bite delivered a surprising saltiness. There was some herb seasoning, which could have been rosemary. I had lived nearly four decades without ever eating or even hearing of *focaccia*, a deprivation that would be hard to replicate today in the States, where countless sins are committed in its name.

Musical finds are another great byproduct of travel, and easier to come by on a trip. Sometimes we hear foreign music first at home, but we don't get the wide range that we do with food. Thai restaurants enjoy a popularity that hasn't carried over to Thai singers. The world music we listen to is often from places—Africa, for instance—that we don't visit as readily as we do Europe, whose non-English language songs we rarely hear. No American network televises the Eurovision song contest, even though most of the entries are sung in English. Our tastes in food are much more eclectic than our tastes in music.

We know tango, the music of Buenos Aires, and bossa nova—whose smooth, cool, sophisticated sound speaks to an older, perhaps imaginary, Rio de Janeiro. But we're less familiar with *fado*—the beautiful, yearning, melancholy music of Portugal. We have as part of our own heritage New Orleans jazz and Memphis blues, both of which are preserved in halls and clubs for the delectation of tourists.

One Sunday in Tennessee, searching for something only slightly more contemporary, I went to Al Green's church outside of Memphis. The service was endless, the singing sublime. Green, during his sermon, talked about the people who had come that morning simply out of curiosity. As one of the few non-African-Americans present, I assumed he meant me. I wanted to shout back to him, "I often go to church when I travel!"

And I buy CDs. My collection is full of singers I had never heard of until I visited their countries: Ewa Demarczyk (Poland), Sezen Aksu (Turkey), Lidija Bajuk (Croatia), Khánh Ly (Vietnam), Nana Caymmi (Brazil), Serge Reggiani (France), Mariza (Portugal), Beny Moré (Cuba), Márta Sebestyén (Hungary), Zhanna Bichevskaya (Russia), Mighty Sparrow (Trinidad). Sometimes I can remember exactly where I was when I first heard them: an apartment in Warsaw, a taxi in Selçuk, a craft shop in Korčula, a riverside café in Hué, a record store in Rio. The CDs give me more than musical pleasure; each time I hear the voices, I see the places.

One of the few times I wished I traveled with a tape recorder was in Sweden, at a Midsummer festival in the small town of Rättvik. In a clearing near a lake, men in traditional dress raised a maypole to the accompaniment of fiddles. Children—some haloed in wreaths—danced around the pole as the fiddle bows flew. The national anthem was played, and people sang with quiet conviction: "May I live and die in this Nordic land." Then everyone danced to ancient airs in the lingering light.

The warmth and timelessness of the celebration impressed me deeply, all the more so because they went against the popular image of

Sweden as cold and contemporary. I was given a glimpse of another, less visible side of the country and of how, in travel, the old can be new.

Discovery

One rarely hears this word associated with travel anymore; like "culture shock," it seems to be from another time. The great geographical, geological, scientific discoveries have all been made, or await scholars and experts, not tourists on vacation.

But all travel constitutes a personal discovery, even if it's only of a new band.

The joys of travel sometimes overlap, but they're each distinct. Discovery is the first of the seven that's not inevitable. It's possible—difficult, but not unheard of—to leave your home and come back no more enlightened, informed, or globally aware than when you left it. A few of the folks disembarking from cruise ships—the ones who passed on the shore excursions to hang out by the pool—might fit this description. However, most people—even those for whom travel is mostly relaxation—return enriched.

There is a self-perpetuating aspect at work. Curiosity makes us travel (What lies out there?) and travel makes us curious. You see people doing things and you're not sure why. You come to an intersection and wonder which street to walk down. A traveler's day is filled with questions. "What's north of the department stores on Boulevard Haussmann?" Kate Simon asked in her "uncommon guidebook" to

Paris in 1967, one of a series of guides that raised the form to literary heights it has not come close to reaching since. "South of the Luxembourg Gardens? East of Les Halles? West of the Etoile? What else is there?"

You can't look at a castle without wondering who built it. So you dip into your guidebook which, while extremely common (it's mainly a directory of hotels and restaurants), contains more history than you've read since high school.

In travel, simply looking around is an education. In hot countries where life is lived on the street, you step out of your hotel and are introduced to the ways that people cook and eat, gesture and bargain, groom themselves and discipline their children. (Mysteries that are kept hidden from you in colder climes.) Sometimes, checking out the modern you stumble upon the traditional. In New Delhi, I walked down steps to see the subway and found on the wall a list of rules, one of which forbade passengers from riding on the roof of the cars.

After half a day in a place—especially a foreign country—you've learned more than from all the books and articles you've read. (And this from a travel writer!) Often you're not even aware of it because you're taking it all in visually, without any effort beyond the essential one of watching where you're going.

Also, much of what you're seeing—learning—you have absolutely no clue about. In Asia, especially, I often walk around feeling not just inadequate as a travel writer, but something of a fraud. I seriously question my right to say anything to anyone about a place I find so alien and seemingly unknowable. I peek into the bowls of the people eating at the sidewalk café, unable to identify what's inside. And I ask myself: How can I know what these people are thinking when I don't even know what they're eating?

Then I come home, tell friends about my trip, and realize by their expressions that I know more than they do. Because I've been there, I can write a story.

When I sit down at the computer, however, I've got more than observations. After a few days of getting acclimated in a place, and taking it all in—learning by osmosis—I try to get involved.

I've always claimed that, as a travel writer, my goal is to have an experience that the average tourist doesn't. However, nowadays tourists have experiences that frequently elude me. There are a vast number of educational trips, everything from eco-tours in Costa Rica to cooking schools in Tuscany to wildlife conservation projects in Namibia. Many people also participate in voluntourism, paying good money to spend their vacations teaching English in China or building schools in Peru. Apart from producing feel-good vibes, this type of travel puts tourists in touch with the locals, who are the best source for learning about the contemporary life of a place.

Independent travel that has a theme, even a personal one— searching for ancestors in Ireland, for instance—offers the same benefit. The trip takes on a purpose, and encompasses a quest, an essential component of which is a dependence on others. In asking around about your family, talking to clerks, archivists, publicans, you learn more than genealogy.

A Florida friend of mine returned to Arkansas for a class reunion at Little Rock Central High School. "It's the only building from my childhood," Don once told me, "that didn't get smaller." After the reunion, he and his wife drove to the Mississippi Delta, and then to Alabama, visiting cities made famous by the Civil Rights Movement. He called it their "Chitlins, Chiggers, Cotton, and Kudzu Tour," but his motive was far from frivolous. He wanted to be reeducated about a painful period in our history, and to pay respects. "It was a journey," he said, "that I needed to take."

Today most of my trips, by necessity, have themes. No magazine will send you to Zurich because you want to write about Switzerland. You have to present a story idea, sometimes with characters, a narrative arc, even pre-determined scenes. It is a process that, in a way, dismisses the concept of discovery.

When I was my own editor I would pick a destination, often for no other reason than I had never been there, and go. (After, admittedly, weeks of research.) With a few exceptions—places celebrating anniversaries, cities preparing for Olympics—I never had a plan of attack, a line of questioning, a set itinerary. I arrived with the thought: Let's see what happens. It gave me great freedom, while filling me with doubts.

Although, I usually found a theme, or a theme found me. One summer I flew to Colorado (for the first time) and drove my rental car to Colorado Springs. In the breakfast room of my B&B, a former resident who had returned for a wedding told me that if I was writing about Colorado I had to write about hiking. I demurred, saying I was more interested in people (I hate being told what to write about), and he said, "That's where you'll meet people—on the hiking trails."

I politely thanked him for his advice and drove to Leadville, primarily because it had an old opera house where Oscar Wilde once lectured. (The bookish traveler.) In a bar, I got talking to a young woman who worked for the local newspaper and spent her weekends climbing mountains—specifically those over 14,000 feet, which she referred to as "fourteeners." She and her friends collected them like trophies. She had five.

My next stop was Aspen where, inescapably, I went hiking—with the insider knowledge that I had gone native.

On those occasions when I failed to find a theme, the stories, even if perhaps a bit unfocused, possessed a verisimilitude that assigned-subject stories often lack. And I don't mean that, in their randomness, they more accurately reflected the true nature of travel.

In 2006, a magazine sent me to the Cook Islands as part of a project on global warming. In Rarotonga, and then in Aitutaki, I talked to officials about rising sea levels and the ongoing installation of home cisterns to catch rain water that, because of changing weather patterns, was a more immediate concern. Even when I wasn't interviewing government workers, I brought up global warming (you never know where you might find that coruscating quote). At some point it occurred to me that everyone I talked to was talking about global warming only because they were talking to me. I was doing my job, which was to force the issue.

On Sunday, everything shuts down on the islands so, like everybody else, I went to church. At communion, the wafers and wine were replaced by small squares of coconut meat and shot glasses of coconut water, which were carried down the aisles on wooden trays. I put this in the travel story the magazine allowed me to write for my newspaper; it presented a more faithful portrait.

Nothing informs like participation in the life of a place. Wherever they go, tourists inhabit their own world—one of hotels, restaurants, souvenir shops, museums—and it rarely intersects with that of the locals. Museums are fascinating, instructive, invaluable—you can't imagine going to London without seeing the British Museum, or Paris without visiting the Louvre. But their subject is the past, which has already been discovered.

Knowledge of history is fundamental (you can't understand the present, as they say, if you're ignorant of the past), but the real challenge and thrill of travel is finding out what's happening now: making your own discoveries. To do this tourists have to leave their world, at least for a time, and enter that of the locals, which consists of schools, parks, offices, supermarkets, beauty salons, stadiums, apartment buildings. Some of these places are difficult to gain access to, but that makes any success all the more satisfying.

Contacts, fruits of your active anticipation, can be of great help, so you call them up, which isn't as easy as it sounds. You have to first figure out how to use the phone (or how to adapt yours) and then talk to people you've never met in a language that is not their own at an hour that is, unfailingly, their dinnertime. If you're lucky, they'll have time for coffee.

You can try couchsurfing, which gives you an automatic, speedy entry into a home (as does using Airbnb). It's become a popular practice, made possible by the Internet, though I wonder if its structured ease deprives the connection of some of the beauty that comes from hard-earned serendipity.

In Cappadocia, a few days after I'd said goodbye to the American mother and daughter who'd given me a ride, I called the friend of a friend in Ankara. Azim was a journalist, working in television, and to my surprise he said he would drive down to Ürgüp (several hours), pick me up, and take me back to Ankara, where I could stay with him and his girlfriend for a few days.

One evening, instead of going out, we watched TV. On the news, men in turbans attacked an effigy of Atatürk. This happened somewhere in Germany, Azim told me. The Turks living there, he explained, were for the most part uneducated workers, many of them fundamentalists who sent money home to support the conservative political party. Later we saw a woman getting hounded by reporters; Azim's girlfriend, Tülay, told me that this was a model who had accepted a proposition from an undercover policeman. I told her that, in the States, female officers pose as prostitutes to catch men who are looking for sex. Tülay, impressed, said she would tell her feminist friends.

Watching TV, I was learning volumes. (I had moved far from the world of Pepperidge Farm.) I felt like an incredibly lucky and privileged traveler. In today's world, I would be just another clued-in couchsurfer. But at least I'd be clued-in.

Contacts and couch owners are sometimes invaluable guides, but you can also meet fascinating people by chance. It's often easier for couples, who are viewed as safe, though they're not always desirous of company (a cruel travel paradox). Solitary male travelers are sometimes seen as suspicious (especially in vacation spots, where couples and families predominate), while single females can feel vulnerable, and as a result may keep a low profile. I met a Japanese woman in Turkey, an interesting young artist, who was traveling around in used, baggy clothing—including a floppy hat—that made her look older and less attractive than she was. She told me the outfit kept her from being harassed.

Male travelers rarely have to resort to costuming. We can explore sketchy neighborhoods that, if we were women, we might be reluctant to visit. We can hang out in bars without being bothered. I frequently go to bars, especially in small American towns where there's not much else to do after dinner. European cafés are mostly useless, as people occupy tables in already formed groups. They're designed for socializing with friends, or for tête-a-têtes—not for meeting strangers. The worldwide popularity of the Irish pub has been a great boon to travel writers.

Sitting at bars I've met interesting people, heard good stories, gotten something of the spirit of places. I spent my one evening in Dubois, Wyoming, at the Rustic Pine Tavern talking to outfitters in cowboy hats who taught me, among other things, how to pronounce the town's name: "Dew Boys." Jonathan Raban, sailing down the Mississippi River to write *Old Glory*, stopped in bars with the idea that he'd come across typical Americans and instead, he once complained, found mainly drunks.

The son of a clergyman, he also attended church suppers, getting a good mix of characters.

I once interviewed Raban, and asked him why he rarely wrote about what he ate. (The church suppers were more about the people than they were about the food.) He gave the impression he didn't think it was important. Yet an interest in food often takes us to markets—though less frequently to supermarkets, where the majority of people shop and where the larger stocks of often unidentifiable foodstuffs provide numerous topics of potential conversation. Here again, mere observation is not sufficient.

On a subsequent trip to St. Petersburg, I was invited to dinner by a Russian woman I'd met six years earlier on my first visit. Saida's husband, Igor, met me downtown and we rode the subway away from the center. It was a long ride. When we finally emerged, it was into a world of vast, dilapidated apartment blocks stretching along wide, featureless boulevards. We had left St. Petersburg and arrived in Leningrad.

But the supermarket was beautiful. Igor picked up a few items, one of which—horizontal strips of fat in a vacuum-sealed package—I recognized immediately as bacon. Arriving at the apartment, he handed his shopping bag to Saida and we went into another room, sitting near a poster tracing the lineage of the Russian royal family. Igor explained that, for decades, Russians were never taught much of their history in school because it didn't conform to the Soviet ideal; only now, he said, were people finally starting to learn about the past.

Half an hour later, Saida called us into the kitchen. Bowls of soup rimmed the table, and various dishes occupied the center, including one layered with rashers of raw bacon. It suddenly occurred to me that I hadn't noticed what Updike once called in a short story the "illicit" aroma of bacon cooking. Igor grabbed a slab and gobbled it down while I watched with astonished revulsion. Like jeans in Paris, bacon in Russia was done differently. I wouldn't have known this (and other things) had I not entered a Russian home.

The meal concluded with the singing of folk songs. I sang "When Johnny Comes Marching Home" and then hummed my favorite Bichevskaya tune that, I was told, is about a young man who has a dream about the wind. The wind, Saida explained, is a metaphor for death; the man knows from his dream that he is about to die.

An upbeat American song about war; a morose Russian song about wind.

It took me years to overcome my shyness, the biggest hindrance to meeting people. An illuminating moment came in the bar of my London hotel in 1976 when the Polish barmaid asked me where I was from. I had been sneaking glances at her from afar, but had only dared to ask her for beers. One year later, when Hania came to visit me in Trenton, New Jersey, I shuddered to think—as I do today—of all that my timidity nearly cost me.

I'm more outgoing now than I was then, and I'm bolder on the road than I am at home. I first met Saida at the Anna Akhmatova Museum, where I had approached her for directions and learned that she was a tourist herself, visiting from her hometown in Dagestan. My philosophy is: Even if I make a fool of myself, it will be in front of people I'll never see again. If I do see them again, it will mean my behavior was the opposite of embarrassing. (Though, you have to work at keeping in touch.)

The more you travel, the more you develop an eye, I think, not only for who's approachable, but who's worth approaching. You have little time, and you don't want to end up spending it with bores. In Lafayette, Louisiana, the first night of a Francophone music festival, I was looking for a place to sit and eat my gumbo when I spotted a man who resembled Woody Allen. I asked if I could join him, and quickly learned that he was a frustrated stand-up comic who was working in his father's lumber company. His comedy act had failed, he told me, because no one in Lafayette understood his humor. Mark and I instantly hit it off, and he became my weekend guide to Cajun culture.

It didn't matter that he wasn't a typical Cajun (more like a neurotic New Yorker). The people you meet in your travels are often not representative of the community. For one thing, they have time to hang out and are open to outsiders (which is how you find them) while most normal people are busy at the office and then home with their families. Abroad, the people you end up talking to are usually people who speak English, an ability that, in most countries, sets them apart from the general population. This is not a negative: it's the citizens who stand outside society—often creative, artistic types—who have the best perspective on it, who can often teach you the most.

Festivals are fertile meeting grounds for residents and tourists; most of the time, if you want to meet people, you have to cross over into their world. It doesn't have to be intimidating. Instead of buying stamps with your postcards in the souvenir shop you go to the post office where, waiting in line, you get a real taste—perhaps the first of your trip—of the life of a local (especially if you stand in the line with the people paying bills).

Sporting events are always a good bet, too: a soccer match in Montevideo, hockey in Montreal, cricket in Mumbai, Australian football in Melbourne. The fans around you may be too wrapped up in the action to talk, but simply by being there you're witness to a national passion (and—depending on the teams—a passionate nationalism).

Cultural events provide quieter venues for meeting locals: concerts, art exhibitions, book readings where, if you don't speak the language, your presence will be all the more intriguing.

One evening on Patmos, in a gallery in the hilltop town of Hora, I struck up a conversation with the exhibiting artist, a young woman who invited me to join her and her friends for dinner. Eftychia closed the gallery and the five of us walked to a square that resembled a movie set. We commandeered a table and ordered a feast. I sat across from Sophia, a translator, who told me that Greeks did not help other Greeks. It struck me as an overly harsh statement. I suggested that perhaps things were changing with the younger generation. (*She* seemed awfully nice.) "I don't think so," she replied. "It's written in our DNA." She paused a few seconds to reconsider. "No," she corrected herself. "It's engraved." I had my coruscating quote—one that I was reminded of frequently during the Greek economic crisis, to which a major contributor was rampant tax evasion.

A tough entry for the traveler is into an office. There is no international community of desk surfers. In São Paulo, I visited a friend of a friend who had married into the family that ran Brazil's largest newspaper, *O Estado de S. Paulo*, and I was offered a tour of the newsroom. At first glance, it looked like every newsroom I'd ever seen: a large, low-ceilinged room with offices on the side and cubicles in the middle. In one of the side offices a large man in suspenders smoked a cigar. The cubicle of one of the news editors was decorated with votive cards. (Of Santo Expedito—but still.) A female reporter walked over to a male colleague and massaged his shoulders as he typed, then she leaned over and planted a kiss atop his bald head. I was given a driver to return me to where I was staying, one of the many drivers used, I was told, to take reporters out to cover stories. The visit made the life of an American journalist seem nasty, sexless, and hard.

Funerals are often more revealing of a culture than weddings, though the latter are more enjoyable to attend. In his beautiful essay "Travel and the Sense of Wonder," John Malcolm Brinnin tells of a man he frequently ran across in his journeys: in Scotland, Trieste, Odessa. In Taormina he saw the man again, outside a church, throwing rice at two newlyweds. Brinnin approached and asked the man if he knew the couple. He didn't. "Oh, I go to everything," he explained, "christenings, funerals, weddings. I love to see life happening."

It should be the motto of every traveler. Then we should build on it by crashing the receptions.

I did, unwittingly, in East Jerusalem. It was a wedding party in a hotel near where I was staying. I got no farther than the lobby, which was sprinkled with men in dark suits, smoking and talking. Every once in a while someone would exit the ballroom, providing me with a quick glimpse of a room full of women, movement, and color before the doors closed again. I was about to leave when a waiter arrived from the kitchen, bearing a tray of demitasse cups. He went around the lobby, presenting the tray to every man present, including me, even though it was obvious from my attire that I was not attending the wedding. I had no business being there, yet I was as deserving of coffee, in the waiter's eyes, as any human being. The sexes were separated, but all men were equal.

What you learn from your travels is unquantifiable, and can sometimes seem wasted, because back home it rarely comes up in conversation. It changes who you are, how you see your own country, and how you see the world (sometimes in ways you're not even aware of). Yet travel feeds a reservoir of knowledge that is not massively called upon in everyday life. And because it's rarely tapped, you sometimes forget that it's there. When you remember, you often downplay its importance.

We live in a large, self-regarding country. It's made up of people, P. J. O'Rourke once explained, who fled hardship elsewhere for a better life here and didn't want to revisit the misery they'd left behind. Spoken like a true Irish-American. Every time I came home, I noticed how little curiosity people had about my travels and how few questions even my friends asked me. What I had done was, for some of them, too far removed from their own experience; they didn't ask me anything, I came to realize, because they had no idea what to ask. They had never been abroad themselves, and imagining foreign countries—another way of life—was too much of a stretch. Of course, there was also the possibility that they simply had no interest. From other people, even some newspaper editors, I got the impression that I was viewed as a slacker, someone coming back from a lark—even when I returned from two lean years of observing, and recording, the beginning of the end of communism in Eastern Europe. I was merely, in the eyes of many, someone who had squandered his time in an insignificant place (i.e., a country that was not the USA).

International experience is becoming more valued, but we still have presidential candidates who hide the fact that they speak French. Seen elsewhere as an asset—in most of northern Europe as a given— bilingualism here is viewed as shameful (at least when it's a politician speaking the language of Voltaire). Nicholas Kristof, in his *New York Times* column, has proposed that the semester abroad become a college requirement. Yet many of the students who participate in these programs now do so for the same uninspiring reason that they attend college: It's the thing to do. They improve their foreign language skills, but most of them don't come back fluent. (Fluency is hard to achieve in four months, especially when you chat with friends back home on Facebook and Skype.) They learn about the culture but very few of them immerse themselves in it. Nothing they've seen back home has shown them the benefits of doing so.

Media devoted to travel—magazines, newspaper sections, TV shows, websites—are mainly in the business of providing information, the great bulk of it practical: sights, lodgings, restaurants, spas. It helps in our navigation and enjoyment of the world (treating it a bit like a giant theme park), but not in our engagement with it. It has created a class of idiot sophisticates, people who know a country's best hotels and hottest clubs but are ignorant of the novelist shortlisted for the Nobel, and even, sometimes, the name of the president. And these are the things that the locals you meet will want to talk to you about.

Escapist travel books, often about rustic homes in sunny places, have reinforced the idea of travel as something superficial and sybaritic. They help explain why travel writers are envied but not respected. Few people today are familiar with the works of Robert Byron, Norman Douglas, Gerald Brenan, or Freya Stark, who all followed the sun but with the seriousness of scholars. Patrick Leigh Fermor, not a book club favorite, walked across Europe as Henry James's ideal of "someone on whom nothing is lost"—assimilating languages, religions, history, art and architecture, flora and fauna—and then wove it all together in exalted prose. Lawrence Durrell had a grand time living on Greek islands—he would not have shied away from the label of hedonist—but he was intimately familiar with the language, the history, the mythology, and the culture; he brought a depth of knowledge to his hedonism that made books like *Bitter Lemons* and *Reflections on a Marine Venus* much more than envy-inducing accounts of foreign idylls. It made them important, and timeless.

I knew my days as a travel editor were numbered when my editor at the newspaper started pressuring me to run a syndicated column on celebrity travel. I had spent my career traveling the globe and talking to nobodies (sometimes, as in Greece, harvesting riches); I didn't want to end it publishing inanities from stars.

It saddened me, because I had always thought of the Travel section, like I think of travel, as educational. In a country where less than a third of the population owned a passport, I had been given the phenomenal privilege of seeing the world. It seemed not only just, but imperative, that I share what I learned.

One of the things I learned was how surprised people were (especially Europeans) when told of the small percentage of Americans who possess passports. They found it shocking—and more than a little troubling—that a people who wield so much influence in the world have so little experience in it.

Happily, things are changing. Today's versions of O'Rourke's don't-look-back immigrants not only speak their native language at home, they fly their kids over to spend summers with the relatives. The children of my Polish friends here in the States attend Saturday morning Polish classes, a practice that was almost unheard of a few generations ago, when people were still in a rush to shed the old ways and become like everyone else. Eventually, the stereotype of the monolingual American will be passé. A high school intern at my newspaper chose Northwestern over the University of Chicago because she wanted "a real college experience," but before starting she took a year off to study classical dance in her parents' hometown of Chennai.

Having one's feet in two cultures, especially in the age of globalization, is a great blessing, and not just for the individual. A first-hand familiarity with the world is the one travel joy that has an importance, in a democracy, that goes beyond the personal.

Emotional Connection

Travel suffers from false advertising. Tour operators, vacation companies, cruise lines, hotel chains, bad travel writers constantly depict it as something "adventurous," "exciting," "romantic." While disingenuous, it's understandable: they're in the business of travel, and their job is to sell it to consumers.

As a result of this hype, people who travel often experience disappointment. Though this is a word that rarely comes up in conversations about travel. Friends will tell you of their wonderful trips, and much of the time they're being mostly honest. But they conveniently leave out the train they missed due to miscommunications, and the town that was closed up for a holiday no one told them about. Travel, like football, is best in highlight form.

And people will joyfully tell you about their vacations from hell. The worst trips, travel writers love to say, make the best stories; everybody loves a good tale of woe.

Travel stories are divided, rather religiously, between paradise (a word used promiscuously by travel magazines) and inferno. The stories about so-called heavenly places predominate, at least in written form (since most publications are dependent on advertising), while tales of the hellish generally belong to the oral tradition (though they sometimes make it into books, like the excellent anthology *Bad Trips*). There is very little middle ground. You not only don't read, you rarely hear someone saying, "The trip was so-so." Or, "Something was missing." Or, "I left feeling a little unsatisfied." The buzz about travel is so great, its reputation so stellar, that it has created a fear that any admission of regret will reflect more on the traveler—and his or her deficiencies—than on travel itself.

Readers sometimes say to me: "You always meet the most interesting people when you travel." I tell them: "Not really. I just write about it when I do. Most of the time I'm wandering around lonely and aimless." So, in my own way, I am as guilty as the cliché-mongers of perpetuating the idea of travel as a continuously fascinating activity. In my defense, all writers shape their experiences into an unrepresentative series of highlights; otherwise our stories would be too boring to read.

Travel's ho-hum side doesn't get much publicity. *Condé Nast Traveler* has never printed the "Top Ten Places Where You Won't Feel a Thing." The luxury names that make it onto their fatuous lists often fit that description, though. In travel there is usually an inverse relationship between money and emotion.

In February of 2000, *The New Yorker* published a story by Janet Malcolm about her trip to Russia in search of Anton Chekhov, during which she lost her luggage. The effort to be reunited with her belongings propelled Malcolm out of her tourist shell: It required her to deal with the locals, and introduced a small drama into her journey. The experience made her reflect on travel and how, most of the time, it is an inherently "low-key emotional experience." Most tourists, she noted, are not doing anything adventurous, exciting, or romantic; they are passive observers— visiting landmarks, looking at paintings—and are less engaged in life than they are on a typical Monday at home. It is only when something happens on our journeys—which is, frequently, something going wrong—that we are able to break through the surface of a place. (This is the principle behind the "bad trips, great stories" theory.)

I read Malcolm's observation with the shock of recognition. It was so true and yet so unacknowledged. When we travel—particularly those of us who go alone—we take ourselves out of our lives for a while. This gives us the welcome break from routine, the glorious novelty, the invaluable lessons, but it tends to leave us emotionally flat.

We exit our lives without, usually, entering someone else's. We drift along as if in a dream—finally present in the longed-for place— but also in a void, deprived of company, conversation, connection. Again, this weighs heaviest on the solo traveler. One autumn evening in Genoa, I walked the streets as darkness fell and offices emptied. Perhaps because the scene was one I never get in Florida—crowded sidewalks, a chill in the air, a charged twilight—I thought of Warsaw, walking with Hania on October evenings. I peered into the faces of the women as they passed so close and oblivious to me on their way home to dinners and lovers.

Wistfulness is not the most enjoyable emotion, but for a traveler it's one of the most common.

Travel has been called the saddest pleasure. Sometimes it's sad because of what we see: poverty, misery, hopelessness. Kate Simon, writing in *Mexico: Places and Pleasures* of some of the capital's less reputable attractions, ends the section on a philosophical note: "There is no playfulness in it, nor even much energy, just restlessness and several kinds of desperation and, if the night is cold and damp, the sight will depress you, which you may deserve or even want, if you've come this far."

Often, though, travel is sad because what we see doesn't include us. Much of a travel writer's life, I once wrote, is spent watching other people have fun. Everyone who travels has the same experience; we're all outsiders, excluded from the action. Being left out is never pleasant, but in travel it's even more frustrating because a few days ago you were not just part of a group, of friends or family, you were the envied and celebrated member—the one heading off, as the travel ads put it, for exciting adventures in exotic lands. Oh, if they could see you now.

There are people who don't need other people. David Foster Wallace spent his last days aboard the *MV Zenith* in his cabin, traumatized by the orchestrated "fun" of cruising. The resulting story—"Shipping Out," published in *Harper's* in 1996—is a recognized masterpiece in the "bad trips, great stories" school. Steinbeck, as mentioned earlier, drove coast to coast and back again with surprisingly few encounters, and even fewer real ones. Bill Bryson, the most popular travel writer of the last few decades, clearly has difficulty approaching strangers.

Of course, writers of any kind are never the norm; those of us who write about travel are different from the start, since we usually head out alone. The reason cited most often is freedom from distraction; when you're by yourself, you're more attuned to your surroundings. Less discussed, but just as important, is the fact that, alone, you're also more sensitive. You not only notice your surroundings more clearly, you respond to them more deeply. Smiles and small kindnesses mean more to the unattached traveler than they do to the happy couple. A merchant in Fethiye adds a few extra sweets to your purchase and you're extremely touched, in part because no one has paid any attention to you in days. If you'd been there chatting with a companion, you wouldn't have been so moved; you may not have even been aware. And the merchant quite possibly would not have been inspired like he was by your lonely presence. The solitary traveler not only notices and appreciates, but sometimes elicits compassionate acts.

The burden of loneliness also forces you to seek out people whose company can become vital to your wellbeing. Once on a trip I went days without having a conversation with anyone other than myself, which resulted in dangerously low levels of self-esteem. Everyone around me was talking, gesturing, laughing—what was wrong with me? One morning I headed toward a building with sliding glass doors and the doors refused to open. They seemed to confirm my suspicion that I had ceased to exist.

On my way home from Vietnam, I stopped for a few days in Hong Kong. Vietnam had given me a notebook full of interesting encounters—students would approach and shyly ask if they could practice their English—and touching invitations into homes. Even when I wandered the back streets of Saigon, workmen would stop their hammering and shout hellos. The hospitality and friendliness warmed me immeasurably, especially in a country that, for most Americans, was synonymous with war. In three weeks, I grew extremely attached to the place in a way that I hadn't been sure was possible as a tourist.

Travel in Vietnam in the early nineties wasn't always easy, though, and I was a bit relieved to arrive into the modernity of Hong Kong. That feeling lasted about a day and a half. For my second lunch in the city, I joined three young businessmen at a communal table that had been set up on the sidewalk. To try to engage them, I asked what kind of soup they were eating. They happily told me, in excellent English, then went back to conversing in Cantonese. I ordered their soup. After my bowl arrived, I took my first sip. To my surprise, no one asked how I liked it. There was not a lick of curiosity about the foreigner, not even a half-hearted stab at a mundane courtesy. In traveling from Vietnam to Hong Kong, I had moved from being prized to being invisible.

When I arrived back home, a friend who had lived in Hong Kong explained the behavior: Hong Kong is a small, populous island; residents live on top of one another, and the last thing they want is more people in their lives. So they build walls to shut themselves off from people. As soon as the businessmen had answered my question, the wall went up. It wasn't personal, my friend assured me; it was a necessary defense against human expansion.

A few months later I traveled to Toronto, where I had dinner with the publisher of a travel newsletter. Evelyn mentioned that she had recently been in Hong Kong, and I asked her how she had liked it—hoping, of course, to hear her complain about its coldness. Otherwise, I would bear full responsibility for my unsatisfying visit. In travel as in life (with books, movies, politics), we want other people's opinions to consolidate our own.

"I loved it," Evelyn said, and then proceeded to tell me of the fabulous time she had had there. I expressed surprise, while inwardly admitting defeat (travel's competitive aspect is even greater among travel writers; she had succeeded where I had failed). I told her my impressions of the city: that I had found it self-involved and difficult to penetrate.

She explained that she had had a guide, a young Chinese woman, and after a couple days—the time it took for me to throw in the towel—they became friends. The woman invited Evelyn home to meet her mother and discussed with her the problems she was having with her boyfriend. Evelyn bought her a copy of *Men Are from Mars, Women Are from Venus*. They bonded, and the beauty of that bond colored the way that Evelyn saw Hong Kong.

Having heard her story, I felt much better. Evelyn had an unfair advantage: She was a woman.

Women connect more quickly than men do. They also, to generalize some more, communicate better. If I had had a guide in Hong Kong, male or female, we wouldn't have developed the same close friendship. I wouldn't have shared my personal problems; more pertinently, no guides would have shared their personal problems with me. It would have been a strict, professional relationship of guide and tourist. Women can get to the heart of things, and engage the heart, much more readily than men can. This is their great advantage as travelers, and it more than compensates for any possible reluctance to explore bad neighborhoods and hang out in bars.

People aren't essential for an emotional connection, however. (Take heart, silent men.) In fact, a lot of travel is a search for solitude. A love of nature propels travelers away from crowded cities to forests, rivers, deserts, oceans, and mountains (Colorado's fourteeners). There is a subgenre of travel book—from Peter Matthiessen's *The Snow Leopard* to Joe Kane's *Running the Amazon* to Jon Krakauer's *Into Thin Air*—that treats travel as an expedition (some more meditative than others), and, occasionally, as a test.

A friend and fellow travel writer once told me that he can appreciate a beautiful landscape, but he doesn't feel the urge to immerse himself in it the way he does when he sees a great city. With nature, it's enough for him to stand back and admire. As a mostly urban traveler, I understood him perfectly. Driving around Arizona, I was mesmerized by the mountains—the way their colors changed depending on the time of day—but I was content to see them from afar (often through a windshield).

Years earlier, on the south rim of the Grand Canyon, I drove from one observation point to another, not just for the views, but the reactions of visitors. For me, almost as fascinating as the great hole was its effect on the people who stood at its edge—everyone from the Japanese schoolgirls desirous of a photo with me (or any handy American) to the retired Ohioan reciting Robert Service's *The Ballad of the Northern Lights*. I needed a story, and suspected that my uninformed thoughts on the geological marvel wouldn't be enough. Also, being unaccustomed to the power of nature, I was curious about its influence on others.

A few years later, at Glacier National Park, I took a hike and saw a grizzly foraging on a distant mountainside. On another walk, I encountered a family of mountain goats. An Easterner on my first trip to the Northwest, I was more elated than I'd been at the Grand Canyon, probably because I'd found furry, animate nature.

True nature lovers aren't so fussy. A ranger at Everglades National Park once told me that sometimes after work she drives home, changes out of her uniform, and then comes back to the park—to enjoy it in the evening. This in a place that, while possessing a subtle beauty, has none of the dramatic scenery, or adorable animals, of western parks. The ranger loved everything about the Everglades, even the mosquitos. Their relative absence during our hike distressed her slightly, as she wanted me to see their impressive swarms. She showed me the best place to study the stars when I returned to the park at night. She had fashioned a life in which she didn't need to travel to be transported by landscape. In fact, all she needed to do was to go to work. She seemed the most grounded person in South Florida.

Judging by their photographs, most travelers are taken by sunsets. Scenic towns built next to water, like Oia on Santorini, fill with crowds for the daily dropping of the orb into the sea. Key West has turned the event into a communal celebration, complete with buskers. It's a big deal at the Grand Canyon, too—although, there, people turn their backs to the sun to watch the play of light on the rocks. They do the same at Uluru in Australia, where the high-end tourists enjoy the show with the help of sumptuous tailgate spreads.

Travelers can be moved in unexpected ways. Evelyn Waugh, in "A Pleasure Cruise in 1929," wrote: "I do not think I shall ever forget the sight of Etna at sunset." He described the pink light mixing with grey pastels and confessed: "Nothing I have ever seen in Art or Nature was quite so revolting."

Music also works on our emotions, usually in a positive way. This is another reason to attend concerts. However, often it's the music you stumble upon—like at a Swedish Midsummer festival, or while attending a service—that makes the biggest impression. You enter a St. Petersburg church where a choir on the balcony is singing vespers and your listless spirit, overdosed on sights, is instantly lifted.

In Riga, Latvia, I went to a midday organ concert in the cathedral—no emcee, no introduction, no visible musician—just a sudden eruption of pipes followed by a cascade of baroque. It was pure aural refreshment, in a country where I didn't speak a word, and it brought a feeling of harmony and peace that was the perfect antidote to the traveler's confusion. The city was just entering onto the tourist circuit at the time (2001) and yet it had found a solace for its weary visitors that more experienced capitals lacked.

Art museums can have the same effect on some people, the difference being that you don't get to sit still in them and watch as a parade of paintings pass by. (Something for curators to consider perhaps.) Looking at art is an active, or at least ambulatory—and tiring—kind of passivity. But people with the right sensibilities can have an emotional experience seeing Cézanne's *Still Life with Apples* in the same way that others can feel uplifted gazing at the Temple of the Golden Pavilion. In his memoir, *My Two Polish Grandfathers*, Witold Rybczynski tells of a trip he took to Europe as an architecture student and how, as a great admirer of Le Corbusier at the time, he visited and sketched a number of his buildings, including the Chapel of Notre Dame du Haut in Ronchamp. Yet it was the ancient temples of Greece, seeing in their natural settings the ruins he knew only from photographs (which had cropped out the surroundings), that made the greatest impression on him. Of his encounter with the Parthenon atop the Acropolis he writes: "I had never before been so *moved* by a building."

Lucky, too, is the traveler who can appreciate the art in everyday scenes—streetlife's shimmering tableau vivant. It took me years to get into the Guggenheim and MoMA because every time I took the bus in from New Jersey I couldn't pull myself away from the shows on the sidewalks. New York gave me my love of walking city streets, even though for years I never made it out of midtown. Those dense blocks alone provided endless visual stimulation: the prostitutes who greeted me with soft hisses and defeated faces as soon as I exited Port Authority, the camelhaired lawyers strolling Park Avenue, the yarmulked merchants chatting in the Diamond District, the liveried doormen facing Central Park (which, like the museums, I never entered because of my fear of missing out). I roamed Manhattan hunting for sights I couldn't forget.

I've traveled the world in much the same way, walking and observing. "Grin like a dog and run about through the city," Jan Morris described the activity, riffing on a line from the 59th Psalm. You never know when you'll find gold. "I am a camera," Christopher Isherwood declared in pre-war Berlin, eight decades before the age when everybody *has* a camera. But how many of us see the world the way Isherwood did? A camera puts a barrier between the photographer and the photographed, making it difficult for emotion to seep through.

One of my loveliest memories of Mexico dates back to my first trip there, which I took with Hania in the early nineties. Our last evening in Mexico City, we walked the huge Zócalo and noticed an animated crowd at one end. Approaching, we saw that it was made up mostly of children, who were throwing parachuted figures high above a subway grate. Dozens of toy soldiers rose with an updraft, sailed gracefully through the air (backdropped by the cathedral), and then landed on the pavement a few yards away, where they were instantly scooped up and hurriedly carried back for their next mission. It was all so ingenious—child's play out of a public work—and incongruous, a simple pleasure in a monumental space, that it planted in me an affection for Mexico that, after four subsequent visits, I continue to feel.

Sometimes you can be moved by making yourself part of a tableau vivant: playing *mas*, for instance, at Carnival in Trinidad (get close enough to the trucks carrying the speakers and the vibrations will literally shake your heart), or entering, after weeks on the *camino*, the cathedral city of Santiago de Compostela.

Our pilgrimage arrived in Częstochowa nine days after leaving Warsaw, under a low and sullen sky. Crowds lined the streets for our entry, just as they had in the capital for our exit, but here we were greeted not by cheers but by hard, piercing, meaningful looks. There was a solemnity and purposefulness to the scene that made it even more intense than the sendoff had been. For the people gathered, as for us, the moment had more than a religious significance (even though we marched while chanting the rosary, as anything political had been banned by our leaders). The pilgrimage, and its reception, were a united expression of national aspirations. As a foreigner, I felt unworthy to be the recipient of so much adulation—a boy handed me a bottle of soda, a man presented me with flowers—but on a personal level, it seemed a kind of recognition; not so much of walking 150 miles, but of spending two and a half years in Poland, suffering through the winters, standing in the queues, learning the language (its own kind of punishment), living with Poles through the ordeals of their history. And, of course, marrying one of them—the light of my life. Many Americans have lived and found spouses abroad, but few have received such a loving and public valediction.

Being a resident, I had earned the points toward this reward, but to redeem them I had to become a traveler. (A pilgrim, one of the most venerable types.) The second identity strengthened my already ineradicable ties to the country.

When I started traveling professionally, I was surprised and delighted to find that I could still make emotional connections to places. I discovered this for the first time in Portugal. After having schlepped around Spain (on my first assignment as a travel editor), I met a Dutch woman, Bibi, who introduced me to a poet, Casimiro de Brito, who, in turn, invited me to dinner (this after weeks of solitary meals) and then took me to a dive to hear men singing fado. It was in Lisbon that I discovered the secret of travel writing, which is also the secret of memorable travel: You approximate, as best you can in the short time allotted you, the life of a local. Once back home and writing, I stumbled upon another secret: The *best* trips make the best stories. Although, I had already known this in theory from books like *A Time of Gifts* and *Between the Woods and the Water*, which are nearly as crammed with meaningful encounters as they are with learning.

I divide the places I visit into two types: Those that I find pleasant enough (a part of one's critical skills is the ability to find what's attractive), write about, and then don't think about much; and those that, in some fundamental way, touch me and continue to do so long after my visit. The latter group, in order of appearance in my life, is made up of: Alsace, Poland (both places, interestingly, caught between two behemoths), Portugal, Mexico, Vietnam, Turkey, Lithuania, and Brazil.

For someone who has been to over sixty countries, it would appear to be a surprisingly short list. Its size would seem to support Malcolm's theory of the "low-key emotional experience" of travel; its content, for the most part, my belief that the less visited places often produce the most meaningful trips. In Spain, I toured the guidebook cities—Madrid, Barcelona, Seville—where, not surprisingly, no one was particularly curious about foreigners. I got the feeling that many of the residents had had quite enough of us. Lisbon, off to the side, on the lower edge of the continent, was not besieged and, subsequently, was much more welcoming. Among other things, the Portuguese speak the best English in southern Europe (outside of Gibraltar and Malta). Sevillanos made me feel like a tourist; Lisboners made me feel like a guest.

It's the latter experience that all travelers crave, though by flocking to well-known places—the curse of sightseeing—we often miss out on it. Yet it's attainable, even in glamour cities like Paris, if you can get invited by your waiter to his family's Sunday dinner. That's next to impossible, of course, but a few degrees less if the café is far from the famous boulevards.

Real emotional connection is more than being treated nicely. It's rare, especially for people just passing through, and thus all the more precious when it occurs.

Like most everybody who's been there, I love Italy. I've visited six times since my Latin Clubs trip, and every time I arrive in the country I feel happy, even when taking a train from France—a country I lived in and whose language I speak. "The French," Jean Cocteau once said, "are Italians in a bad mood." (Alsatians are different.) I've had wonderful experiences in Italy (again, like most of the tourists who've been there); I've met good people and, with some of them, I've become friends. Yet I've never felt the emotional bond with Italy that I feel with Vietnam and Turkey, possibly because there are so many people vying for her affections. She is the most popular girl in school, which creates a distance, even if it's only in the minds of her admirers. I love Italy, but I've never gotten the feeling that Italy loves me back.

Loving the unloved, you naturally assume the feeling is mutual.

You may be wrong—as travelers often are, in so many ways, about so many things—but it doesn't change the nature of your affection, or your relationship with the couple you got talking to at the post office who invited you to their home, cooked you dinner, refilled your glass, and told you stories of life under a dictatorship. At the end of the night, they insisted on escorting you back to your hotel, where you exchanged phone numbers and email addresses. At that moment, the place stopped being just the site of your vacation; it became the home of your friends. It took on a significance, and entered your heart.

Heightened Appreciation of Home

This joy is felt most intensely while traveling, a time when, ideally, you're not supposed to be thinking about home. You're expected to be preoccupied with the new, fully immersed in the moment.

Where have I been? In the age of multitasking, total immersion seems an antiquated concept. Concentrating on a single thing is a near impossibility at home, why would we ever attempt it on the road? Technology has provided us with endless distractions and numerous ways to brag about our trips. We can post pictures, text updates, tweet sweet nothings—activities that, while impressing friends (and making others jealous), successfully take our minds off the fact that we're not really experiencing the moment we're recording.

Today's traveler is, or at least can be, forever in touch with home. In *Dark Star Safari*, published in 2003, Paul Theroux boasted about traveling the length of Africa disconnected. "People said, 'Get a cell phone, use FedEx, sign up for Hotmail, stop in at Internet cafés, visit my Web site . . .'

"I said no thanks. The whole point of my leaving was to escape this stuff, to be out of touch."

A few years later, riding the rails across Europe and Asia, he carried a cell phone.

Connection with home makes travel more reassuring and less intense. (Though that's only one reason why *Ghost Train to the Eastern Star* is inferior to *The Great Railway Bazaar*.) I felt depressed when I arrived at my dorm room in Provence, and thought of all the people I would not see or hear from for months. It was my introduction to the saddest pleasure. Traveling solo in the seventies didn't ensure total immersion—you could always hang out with expats, speak your own language—but it did guarantee total separation. Friends and loved ones had, unanimously, departed the scene.

This made total immersion a logical option; instead of wallowing in homesickness, you wrapped yourself in your surroundings.

After nine months in Provence, I was a different person. Had Facebook and Skype existed then, the change would have been a lot less dramatic—and my French less proficient—because I would have spent a fair amount of my time engaged in former practices, cliques, mindsets. (And parochial ones at that, since none of my friends were doing what I was.) My new life would have been pock-marked by incursions from my old one. Technology's ability to keep us connected would have hampered my growth.

When I arrived on the farm in Alsace, the pleasure of an entirely new persona was heightened by the secrecy: No one I knew had any clue where I was or what I was doing. My parents, who were aware that the school year had ended in Provence, had to wait for an aerogram to receive the news that their son was milking cows.

Except during their visit in February, I didn't speak to my parents for a year. It was not just the expense of a telephone call, but the imponderableness; talking to my parents in New Jersey, while sitting in Alsace (or Provence), would have been disruptive, discon-certing, absurd, a kind of sacrilege. It shows how large the world was in those days, and how self-enclosed and detached its manifold parts, which made moving through them a challenging thrill. It also illustrates a truth about travel that I think still holds: the farther you get from home—not just geographically, but emotionally—the clearer you see it.

Rudyard Kipling famously wrote, "And what should they know of England who only England know?" Kipling lived before the advent of instant communication, but in an age that had, instead of social media, social institutions, which did more than provide a distraction, they offered a refuge. An Englishman posted to the tropics could continue to live as if he were still in England, going to the club in the evening to read *Punch*, drink gin, and talk about the weather (having exchanged a monotony of rain for a monotony of heat). He could play cricket on the maidan (or padang, or savannah). During the sweltering summer months he could repair to a hill station and be soothed by fake Tudor mansions, wild rose bushes, and afternoon tea. A comforting facsimile of home had been meticulously constructed to protect him from the Other.

Kipling, whatever criticisms one might have of him, was not a stranger to the Other. Having been born in India, and sent to school in England, he experienced firsthand the curious duality of travel: that it teaches us about home while teaching us about the world. Some contemporary writers have expanded (or contracted) this idea to show how, by traveling, we learn about ourselves. Pico Iyer (born in England to Indian parents who moved to California and sent him to Eton) has deftly flipped this self-absorption and reminded us how, as travelers, we educate the people we meet (even if we're unaware of it) about the places we live. And quite possibly what they learn from us, to carry the process one step further, makes them reflect on where they live. Travel, ideally, is both learning and teaching, and the lessons are divided between there and here.

If *here* is one of the blessed places on Earth, the insight feeds gratitude.

Though not for everything. Even before arriving *there* we can sometimes be reminded of our deficiencies, especially if we're traveling from the East Coast across the Pacific and fly an American airline to California, and then an Asian one the rest of the way. The smiling faces on the latter plane, the obsequious service, come as a shock (the first of many) and seem to hark back to an earlier, more gracious age of travel. (As well as, some might rightly add, a time of unquestioned sexism and ageism.)

Traveling around almost any industrialized country, we're made painfully aware of the inadequacy of American public transportation. Trains in Europe and Japan make Amtrak look like something from the last century (which it is). On the other hand, Europeans who rent cars in the States are always impressed by how long our freight trains are.

The journalist T. R. Reid took his bum shoulder to a number of countries to experience and study their health care systems—a journey that, unsurprisingly, didn't reflect favorably on the United States. (France, he concluded, had found the best way to look after its citizens.)

On a less critical, yet connected, note, we often find we eat better abroad. It's not just that we're introduced to new tastes (as mentioned earlier), but that we're reacquainted with old ones. Eating breakfast once with a group of Texans in Brazil, I heard everyone voice enthusiasm for the fried eggs. They tasted like eggs.

A few years ago, *The New York Times* identified changes in travel types: The Chinese were the new Japanese (going in groups, cameras in hand); the Russians were the new Arabs (flashy and flush); and Americans were the new Germans, painfully aware of being unloved and, as a result, keeping a low profile. All the characterizations struck me as accurate. Although we may not have realized it, we have long traveled under an onus; it is so much easier to go out into the world when your entire nationality has never been labeled "ugly." The Americans I've met in my travels over the last several years have been, for the most part, very respectful of other cultures; there's much less of the "that's-not-how-we-do-things-at-home" attitude than there used to be. This is partly due to education; we seem to be more curious and better-informed than in the past (slowly catching up with the Germans). However, it's also the result of the unique and changing nature of our country, made up of people from everywhere who, instead of shedding, now embrace their ethnicity. A nation that celebrates diversity is, inevitably, going to produce sensitive travelers.

(The English, *The Times* claimed, were the new Americans, loud and obnoxious.)

Although we can still be boisterous, something that becomes apparent in sotto-voiced Europe. It could be seen as part of our charm, but usually isn't. My parents, who were not loudmouths, seemed almost to bellow when they visited me in Poland—a country where people had learned, for obvious reasons, to speak in low, non-carrying voices.

The day they came to pick me up from the *Stefan Batory*, and we drove from Montreal back to New Jersey, I listened amazed as almost every commercial on the radio was not only loud but all about money. "Big sales!" "Huge savings!" "Money back guarantees!" "No money down!" I had just returned from a country where, for two years, I had never heard a discussion about money. Nobody had it so nobody talked about it. I knew that Calvin Coolidge had said, "The business of America is business," but it took living under a socialist system for me to see how obsessed we are with moola.

There's a hush in France as well, even while eating—an ambiance that makes American restaurants, with their pounding music and uninhibited cacklers, a kind of torture for visiting Europeans. Contributing to the Gallic calm are Gallic children, who, from an early age, are treated as small adults. This is noteworthy to Americans who sometimes seem to aspire—we men particularly—to an eternal adolescence. "The American male," wrote Wilfred Sheed (who as a child was shuttled back and forth between England and the US) "doesn't mature until he has exhausted all other possibilities." The French approach makes being a kid tough, I suppose, but it produces tough, responsible kids. A few of these children invariably grow up to become celebrity intellectuals, a status that is hard to imagine in the US. Books about French child-rearing philosophies—as well as diet strategies—have appeared in English, written by Americans with experience living in France; our unwavering belief in French superiority has moved beyond the fields of gastronomy and fashion. Unfortunately, it hasn't reached the health care realm.

For my student Christmas in France, I was invited by a freshman to her hometown of Perpignan. One evening we went out with her friends, one of whom looked up at the moon as we walked down the street and asked if I felt proud that an American flag now stood on it. The question caught me by surprise. Like everyone else I knew, I had been excited by the moon landing a few years earlier, and delighted that we beat the Russians to it. (My American adolescent competitiveness?) But I didn't look at the moon, as this young Frenchman did, and think of American prowess.

That evening brought home to me something that I have struggled with ever since. I am a small, low key person who ekes out a modest living as a writer. Yet when I travel, passport in hand, I represent the richest, most powerful country in the world. I see myself one way while appearing to people through a completely different—in fact, opposite—set of personality traits. At least initially, who I am gets completely distorted by what I am. (Although in certain countries, I authentically become rich in comparison to most of the population.)

Some people might revel in a changed image, travel becoming for them a way to escape their insignificance and take on, simply through their nationality, perceived super powers. But I have always been concerned about it. Being an American abroad seems to conflict with my love of the underdog which, at home, I come by naturally.

I have been both a victim and a beneficiary of national stereotyping. One evening I was eating in the university cafeteria in

Provence when a French student approached and asked if the seat beside me was empty. I told him it was. "American," he said disdainfully on hearing my accent, before heading off to find another table. It was not long after the end of the Vietnam War, when many *American* students were feeling anti-American. That was the only such slight I experienced all year; most people were smart enough to differentiate between the individual and his government.

A few years later in Greece, I got a taste of Hellenic anti-Americanism. I had arrived on the Iron Curtain Local—three months after the murder of the CIA's bureau chief in Athens—and found a job teaching English in the northern town of Arta. The director was less than delighted to see me (I had been sent by the main office in the capital). In addition to my weekday classes, he assigned me one hour on Saturday evening, neatly squashing any chance of my ever going away for the weekend.

It was a rude shock after Poland, which had a deep (and sadly unrequited) love for the United States. In those years, all Westerners enjoyed a special status in Poland. We were seen as emissaries from a world the Poles knew themselves to be a part of but, through circumstances beyond their control (the names Roosevelt and Yalta came up in conversations with disturbing regularity), they had been cut off from. Of all the Westerners, Americans, despite our perceived role in their malaise, received preferential treatment.

I suspected that whatever disappointment Hania's relatives might have had in me as a man, it was made up for by my being an American.

For many Poles, we came from what was still the Land of Extraordinary Opportunity. My students were bemused, if not dumbfounded, by the fact that I had come from America to teach them English. (They were more comprehending when they learned that a woman had been behind the move.) During the two and a half years I taught at the school, a few of the teachers left to find work in the States; this made a lot more sense to everyone. A Polish friend told me that she once saw a man waiting for a train and knew immediately that he was an American, not by what he wore, but by how he sat. "*Siedział tak pewny siebie*," she described it. ("He sat so self-assured.")

More importantly, Americans came from the Land of the Free. It is difficult to truly appreciate the great privilege of voting unless you spend time in an authoritative state. It's hard to grasp the magnificence of a phrase like "freedom of speech" if you've never lived in a country that denies it. Poles spoke very openly in private, and sometimes even when standing in queues for food, but it was not always prudent, as evidenced by the fact that I—of all people—was asked to become an informer. Hania found this more amusing than sinister, but I'm not sure I've ever felt so far removed from the world I knew. My life in New Jersey had never resembled a John le Carré novel. Even though the man who tried to recruit me insisted that—by coming to his office once a week, and reporting what people were saying—I would be doing work very similar to the journalism I had practiced in the States. It was an analogy that, had I not been so stunned, would have made me laugh in his face.

Even though the regime in Poland was never as harsh as it was in the Soviet Union, or in East Germany, it created a wariness among strangers that made the friendly, easy-going banter of Americans almost nonexistent. Toward the end of my stay, I saw a cashier in a store chatting amicably with an elderly hanger-on and realized with a shock that I had not seen such an exchange during my time in Warsaw.

Americans—you realize when you travel, especially in old, decorous Europe—have taken freedom of speech and run with it. It's as if *because* we can say what we want, we *do*—to pretty much anyone who will listen. We spill not only our thoughts, but our desires, fears, loves, hates, personal histories (though, oddly in a country obsessed with money, not our incomes). There are not that many countries in the world where you can sit next to a stranger on a bus and hear, in the course of the journey, the story of his life. Even if the bus is just going cross-town. Some folks find this irritating; travel writers are not among them.

In Warsaw, people didn't smile on the street; there wasn't a lot to smile about. Even if there had been, the expression would have been saved for people who mattered. Europeans find our cheerfulness facile and insincere. In Paris, according to Olivier Magny, author of *Stuff Parisians Like*, the smiling American is regarded as something of an idiot. An intelligent person, i.e., a Parisian, knows that life is tragic and doesn't pretend otherwise. But there is an ease and pleasantness in being among sunny people, even if many of them are on medication.

It was not just the system but the weather that affected Poles' moods. In winter, the sun—which you often didn't see for a week—set in mid-afternoon. It was like living at the bottom of a large aquarium, and it made New Jersey winters seem almost sparkling. Today, Poland is democratic and the economy is stable, but the weather hasn't changed, and an ancient fatalism persists. An American friend who worked in Prague in the early nineties told me that, during his time there, he missed our "can-do" spirit.

In those years I grew nostalgic for American sports, because whenever I found a game on TV it was women's handball from Łódź. At least it always seemed to be. Americans coming upon Eurosport in their hotel rooms are surprised—even the most rabid fans—by how many uninteresting sports exist. One crisp October evening in Warsaw, as I sprinted across the boulevard near our apartment, I thrust out my arms and imagined a perfect spiral falling into my homesick hands.

I had an English friend in Warsaw who had been a student at the university and had married a Mexican who worked at her country's embassy. Living like a diplomat, he had a cushy life, protected from the shortages and the queues that the rest of us endured. Still, some things eluded him as they did everyone else. "What Warsaw needs," Andy used to say, "is a good Italian restaurant."

Or, I thought, a good Italian neighborhood. During my first stroll around Warsaw in 1978, I realized after a few hours that the city was pretty much devoid of immigrants (which I must have known, without somehow considering the consequences). Wherever I went, I found only Poles. The absence of an Irish section or a Hispanic neighborhood or a Chinatown was as dispiriting, to an American, as the socialist architecture and the frumpy mannequins and the doleful shop assistants. I eventually came to love Warsaw—its dark humor, its resilient spirit—but I often thought longingly of Philadelphia.

Americans, especially urban ones, can go to most places in the world and find them more homogeneous than the ones we've just left. At first, it doesn't hit us because the whole scene is so new. We walk down a street in Kyoto and we're mesmerized by the crowds, the signs, the lights, the bustle, which is not at all what we expected in the city of temples. After a few days, however, we notice that the sidewalks churn with black-haired heads. The blondes mixed in are clearly tourists; the purple 'do is obviously dyed. In the strange land is a strange uniformity.

It is one of the ironies of travel for Americans: In pursuit of the foreign we're often shown, by comparison, how much of it we have here at home. And it occurs to us, particularly while traveling through more traditional societies, how the vast majority of us are fine with that. In another irony, the activity that is famously "fatal"—in Mark Twain's words—"to prejudice, bigotry, and narrow-mindedness," shows us how relatively tolerant we are.

Americans who go abroad today discover that we're not so much the nation that put a man on the moon, but the one that elected an African-American president. Twice. We are the country where same-sex couples are not only accepted but given rights. (Russia, by contrast, banned Gay Pride parades for the remainder of the twenty-first century.) We argue over whether it's possible for women to have it all while their counterparts in Saudi Arabia aren't even allowed to drive. Saudi women *can* now participate in the

Olympics, where they face the challenge, like the rest of the world's women, of competing against beneficiaries of Title IX, which prohibited gender-based discrimination in educational institutions forty years *before* Saudi Arabia—and Qatar and Brunei—finally agreed to send their female athletes to the games. A large number of countries demonstrate to us how inclusive, and uncommon, our belief in equal opportunity is.

European elevators (and bathrooms) reveal the luxury of American roominess (which we generally take for granted). Many places outside Europe show us, through dented cars and littered lots, how comfortable (for the most part) and well-kempt we are. Residents of Boston and South Florida can feel—on the streets of India, or even Italy—unprecedented warmth toward their hometown drivers.

Every traveler is familiar with the beauty of homecoming, though the assumption is that it's greater for people returning from disasters, or (undeclared) nonevents: Thank God that's over. However, the sweetness of return is felt even by the traveler who is reluctant to leave.

The backseat of the taxi becomes a zone of contentment. You gaze out the window at the once daunting city, now beloved and irreplaceable. You grab your bags (heavier than before) and part with the last of your colorful bills. The terminal doors slide open, and then close behind you; now nothing can touch the precious memory of your visit. You breathe in the neutral air of an international airport. The last time you inhaled it you were a clueless foreigner; today, you're the accomplished traveler. The woman at check-in speaks perfect English.

Waiting in lines, you talk to everyone—you're all at the same unreal time in your lives—and find that their trips were as excellent as yours was. The world appears to be made up of travelers, and the travelers are all people you'd like to have as friends. With a few of them, you exchange cards.

Hours later, you exit customs wearing the rumpled look of the returning hero (visible to any loved ones waiting). The cars on the highway seem to move aside for your passage.

You arrive at your house (or apartment or condo) and find it more beautiful than your five-star hotel—or the dream you had of it on the tenement couch. Here are your pictures, your books, the freezer holding ice cubes, the TV showing baseball, the alarm clock you know how to set. There is mail stacked up and even the junk is calling your name. You reunite with the shower. Finally, you climb into bed—your bed—and the feeling of security is saturated with thankfulness.

Stories

Warsaw Redux

I have never read, let alone written, a travel story about the period before the travel. The closest things to it would be those articles you find in newspapers and magazines containing tips on booking hotels, packing, avoiding jet lag (ha!)—all the practical aspects of trip preparation that sometimes enhance, but more often dampen, the pleasure of anticipation.

This story about my return to Warsaw in 2011, three decades after I lived and worked there, describes a city that Poles had been waiting for since the start of the Second World War in 1939. When the war and the Nazi occupation ended six years later, Warsaw, like the rest of the country, found itself part of the Soviet Bloc, a situation that lasted until 1989. It took a while, in newly democratic Poland, for the capital to come into its own, but Warsaw is accustomed to rebirths, just as its citizens are to waiting for them. I got a small taste of what they had been through when I was finally able to visit—after years of wanting to—an unusually meaningful institution.

In summer, Warsaw smells of linden trees. The remembered scent greeted me promptly, as even the street leading in from the airport is lush with leaves. They help soften the blow of gray apartment blocks.

Jurek parked in front of one such building on a tree-lined boulevard in the neighborhood of Mokotów. We took the small elevator up to the third floor, where his wife Monika greeted me warmly. In the kitchen, supper was laid out on the table and the windows were open to a view of the prison. Gazing out I thought, as I always do when taking in that scene: what a strange place for one's wife to have been born.

~

April 6, 1952. The previous year, Halina Matraś had been accused of espionage on behalf of the Polish government-in-exile and, though pregnant, sentenced to ten years in Mokotów Prison. That summer, her sister came to take the three-month-old baby away. Little Hania looked so sickly that, on the tram, outraged mothers hurled abuse at her aunt. Halina was released after five years, during a period of de-Stalinization, but those five years took a heavy toll.

~

I learned some of this when I met Hania in London in the summer of '76, and more when I came to Warsaw two years later—a few days before her mother died. One of the last things to make her mother laugh was the story of my going to the store to buy water and coming back with a bottle of clear vinegar.

More successful at job hunting, I found work as an English teacher. After six months, my visa expired. When I requested an extension, I was asked to become an informer. (My own small, sour taste of the regime.) I refused, which meant quitting my job and leaving the country. However, thanks to the birth of Solidarity, I was able to return in the fall of 1980. Hania and I were married that October in the Old Town, and I stayed for two years—teaching English, learning Polish, and gathering material for my first book.

~

In the morning, the guard gazed out from his corner tower. Over breakfast I told Jurek—Hania's cousin—of my desire to visit the prison. Hania had gotten in touch with a retired professor who had written a book about female political prisoners, and had been a prisoner herself. Jurek, to my surprise, thought that a visit wouldn't be impossible. More immediately, he said, there was an event in the park next to the Hotel Bristol, as today marked the twenty-second anniversary of the first free postwar elections. Like the scent of linden trees, the Polish passion for remembrance came back to me.

The Bristol—Warsaw's most elegant hotel—sits, appropriately, on its stateliest street. In the early eighties, I had used Krakowskie Przedmieście—with its reconstituted grandeur—as a refuge from the drab, dilapidated city beyond. Leveled by the Nazis, Warsaw was rebuilt by the Communists—about as horrible a fate as any city could have. Though the Old Town, and my favorite street, were painstakingly made to look their former selves.

On recent visits, having seen more cities, I had begun to think of Krakowskie Przedmieście as possibly the world's most perfect street. It is infinitely cozier than Fifth Avenue, and much more varied than the regimented Champs-Élysées. In the space of only a few blocks, it contains all the classic elements of a great urban boulevard: shops, galleries, bookstores, restaurants, cafes, gracious apartment houses, baroque and neoclassical churches, historic palaces (including the president's), a grand hotel, a fine university, diminutive parks, and heroic statuary honoring, among others, a prince, a poet, and an astronomer. Krakowskie Przedmieście is more than a thoroughfare; it is a capital, and a culture, distilled to their essence.

On this bright June afternoon, it looked better than ever. (The nostalgia that normally accompanies a return to a former home is magnificently tempered when that home was formerly Communist.) I walked with summery crowds past sidewalk cafes in a soothing but puzzling calm—until I realized that there was no traffic. The perfect street had found the perfect solution (at least for the weekend).

The park next to the Bristol was furnished with poster boards, and tables of books, devoted to the distant late twentieth century. Mock voting stations had been set up in honor of the anniversary; I grabbed a ballot that asked if fans should be allowed to attend an upcoming soccer tournament. It was cheering evidence that the national delight in absurdity—an essential in the past for keeping one's sanity—had not disappeared. I checked "*Nie*" and dropped my ballet in the box.

A small bookstore behind the hotel sold postcards with black-and-white scenes from the Polish People's Republic. There were now guidebooks devoted to walking tours of old Communist-era landmarks, and I found it encouraging that enough time had passed for Poles to acknowledge (if not embrace) the vestiges of that time. One postcard showed three peasants in overcoats, each holding a piglet. I bought it to send to Hania, who, because of work, had been unable to come.

Heading toward the Old Town, I came across a bench with a button at one end. I pushed the button and unleashed the "Grand Polonaise Brillante, Op. 22." The writing on the bench, in Polish and English, informed me that it had been from the building across the street, in 1830, that Fryderyk Chopin had left Warsaw on a stage-coach to Vienna, "never to return."

Krakowskie Przedmieście—its treasures now with musical accompaniment—began its descent into Plac Zamkowy (Castle Square). Protestors clamored around King Sigismund's column, speaking through megaphones and waving Syrian flags. Asking around, I learned that almost all of them had come to Poland as students and decided to stay. They provided a new twist on an old theme—"*Niech żyje Syria!*" they chanted, "Long live Syria!"—as well as proof of Warsaw's international status.

~

Noemi sat at a sidewalk café on Plac Konstytucji—a monumental, Stalinist-era square now softened by umbrellas. Even its reliefs of heroic workers and teachers had taken on a kind of period charm now that the ideology behind them had been sent packing.

Noemi had dark hair, brown eyes, and almost unaccented English. She had recently graduated from Jacek Kuroń High School—a private institution named for one of Solidarity's leading lights. There had been sixteen students in her graduating class. Now she was looking for a summer job, not abroad—as generations of Poles, like Hania, had done—but in her hometown.

"I used to hate Warsaw," she said, with that universal teenage belief in the superiority of elsewhere. "Then I went to Ottawa. The grass," she said with disgust, "was cut so perfectly."

She reflected for a moment, then continued. "Warsaw might be a mess, people may be angry, but they say what they think." I thought of the mothers berating Hania's aunt on the tram. "They don't care what people think of them."

She sipped her strawberry smoothie, sitting in an armchair that looked as if it were on loan from a prewar apartment. She told me, as if revealing something shocking: "Young people don't read. I read and

I'm a weirdo." When I asked about the then new Copernicus Science Center, she told me matter-of-factly about the exhibit that indicates which sexual position is best for use inside a small Polish Fiat.

Then, before heading off on her job search, she invited me home to meet her parents. "Polish hospitality," she said smiling.

But I had a full plate. The following day I met Kasia, the daughter of friends in Philadelphia. The country's robust economy had brought back quite a few Poles who had immigrated; in this family's case it was the children—both Kasia and her sister—not the parents who had returned (at least for a while).

We walked down Próżna Street, past the last brick buildings of the old Jewish Ghetto. We crossed Plac Grzybowski, whose unruly grass made me think of Noemi. We visited Nożyk Synagogue—the only temple in Warsaw to survive the war.

Kasia told me about the organization she had started, Forum for Social Diversity, whose challenging mission was to make tolerance in Polish society mainstream. With her American upbringing, Kasia was accustomed to being with people from different countries, cultures, and religions. This type of experience was new to most Poles, who lived in a predominantly Catholic, and ethnically monotone, country that traditionally *produced* immigrants. However, now, with Poland's healthy economy on a continent in crisis, it was receiving them. (Ukrainians and Vietnamese being the most numerous.) She had recently been working with the Ministry of Internal Affairs as it attempted to implement a strategy on immigration.

We stopped for lunch at Chłodna 25. The café had a familiar look: mismatched furniture, T-shirted staff, laptops-in-residence. Yet its renunciation of slickness was perhaps more crucial here because, as Kasia said, "Warsaw is still in a transition period." Foreign chains continued to move in, threatening the existence of places like this. Kasia mentioned that the cafe often hosted events: readings, discussions, exhibits. "It's a model," she said, "for those who do socially-conscious businesses."

After lunch, we met two of my friends for a tour of Praga. Joasia was an artist who had recently moved from Krakow to be with Jason, a translator originally from Austin, Texas. Praga is a working-class neighborhood on the other side of the Vistula River, long famous for drunks and now popular with artists.

The tram rumbled east across the Poniatowski Bridge. Joasia told me that she sometimes felt homesick for Krakow—its beauty and compactness—but that she was enjoying the clean air of Warsaw.

"And there are a lot more things happening here."

We changed trams, ending up eventually at Fabryka Soho: a former factory now housing offices, studios, and exhibition spaces. A bus—Jason had the routes down pat—took us to Fabryka Wódek, an old distillery now peppered with galleries and studios. At one point we passed the gates of the old Bazar Różyckiego where Hania and I, and many Varsovians, used to hunt for Western goods—food, clothing, household items—unavailable in the shops.

We wandered ignored down supposedly mean streets, ducking occasionally into Dickensian courtyards. One had been turned into a bar—with trees in huge pots—and christened Sen Pszczoły (Bees' Dream). Tonight it was showing the multi-media works of student artists. Their professor gave a short speech, and then kissed the hands of all of the females.

"In Krakow," Joasia said, impressed, "students kiss professors' hands."

~

The next morning, I went to see Barbara Otwinowska—the professor with whom Hania had been corresponding. She lived on the eleventh floor of an eyesore at the edge of the Old Town. Her apartment was a cramped space lined with bookshelves and hung with oil paintings, as well as a large mirror in an ornate gold frame. Like the apartments of many older Varsovians, it was a rich representation of a rudely circumscribed life.

The professor showed me a copy of her book on female political prisoners. Walking past the prison a few days earlier, I had stopped to read the plaque on the wall. Warsaw is a city of plaques, the majority commemorating victims of war and totalitarianism. They are ubiquitous, everyday reminders—often brightened with flowers—of the immense suffering that has been inflicted on this place. And they make one appreciate, in a way, the charmless (if leafy) neighborhoods outside the center. For if all of Warsaw looked like Krakowskie Przedmieście—if the city possessed the unbroken beauty of Paris—it would be difficult to believe in its brave and tortured past. The gray apartment blocks are their own kind of memorial.

The large plaque on the prison wall carried the names of the people who had died inside during "the years of Communist terror ... 1945-1955." The date of its unveiling was 1992.

Now I sat at the professor's book-piled table, eating lemon sorbet while she read the letter I had brought from Hania. When she finished, she said that she knew a man at the Ministry of Justice who might be able to get us into the prison.

~

Jurek and Monika were leaving for vacation, so I moved to a hotel on Krakowskie Przedmieście—exchanging a view of a guard tower for one of fairytale rooftops. Downstairs there was a notice of a book reading—my hotel was Dom Literatury (Literature House)—starting shortly in the Museum of Literature on the Old Town Market Square.

Tour groups scuffed the cobblestones of Świętojańska street. Because it was rebuilt, the Old Town is sometimes criticized for being Disneyesque. Such complaints usually come from people who have never seen it deserted on a winter's night. It is an exquisitely detailed, faithfully rendered, and now well-worn replica of the original. It is long past its days as the commercial heart of the city, so

101

it has the feel more of an attraction than of a vibrant urban center. But it is far from being what one might call plastic.

In a crowded room overlooking the square, Jacek Moskwa spoke about his biography of Pope John Paul II. The beloved actress Maja Komorowska read dramatic excerpts. The filmmaker Krzysztof Zanussi listened in the back. It was like an old Catholic intelligentsia meeting.

Czesław Bielecki arrived for the reception. A renowned and often reviled architect, and former mayoral candidate, he had also been a resident—in '68, and again in the eighties—of Mokotów Prison. When I told him that I was writing an article about his city, he announced in characteristically hyperbolic fashion: "Warsaw is the ugliest capital in Europe."

~

"I would agree with that," Filip said quietly when I fed him the line. "But it's got its own charms."

We were having breakfast at Charlotte—a bright café on Plac Zbawiciela next door to the English Language College where I used to teach. I had seen it a few days earlier when I had visited the school and met with Jolanta, the daughter of the headmaster who had hired me in 1978. Back then the school had two thousand students; today, according to Jolanta, it has 350. Language schools now dot the city, while in the seventies and eighties the English Language College was the only private school teaching English, and the only place Poles could learn to speak it with a New York Jewish accent. (On Fridays, I played tapes of Woody Allen's old stand-up routines.)

I knew Filip's father, a photographer who had grown up in England and moved to Poland in the 1970s—a propitious time for photojournalists in Eastern Europe. In fact, in 1981 he took the iconic photograph of martial law: a tank parked in the snow in front of Moscow Cinema which was advertising the film *Apocalypse Now*.

His son had gone into the writing side of journalism, and was now a magazine editor. He had not only studied but worked abroad, and he spoke English with a British accent. I asked him why he lived in Warsaw.

"It's an easy life," he said. "It's much more comfortable than in New York or London. And it's cheaper. You can afford so much more. You can go out every night." (The words of a man with a good job in publishing; pensioners were a lot less sanguine.)

Filip admitted that Krakow had better nightlife. In Warsaw, he told me, you always went to the same places: Powiśle, for instance, the converted ticket hall under the Poniatowski Bridge. "Practically every night you end up here on Plac Zbawiciela." Upstairs from Charlotte was the club Plan B, though it was hard for me to think of my old school's square (really a circle) as constituting "the scene."

On his way to the office—it was now after ten—Filip dropped me at the Copernicus Science Center on the banks of the Vistula. Inside, crowds of excited children pulled at contraptions, excavated for artifacts, and listened to the voice of an electronic poet (based on a character in a Stanisław Lem novel). The place had more of the air of a funhouse than of a museum. After some searching, I found the interior of a small car built into a wall; taking a seat and pressing buttons, I heard forthright answers to questions about human reproduction. Jurek had told me that the government wanted to get more young people studying hard sciences, as subjects like sociology had become popular. It struck me that it was not only the museum's interactive aspect that was novel, but its focus on the future.

In the evening, back in the city center, I walked into the whirl that is U Kucharzy (Chez the Chefs). The name was appropriate, because the restaurant was housed in the former kitchen of the Europejski Hotel. I knew the place well; Hania and I had eaten a sad dinner there on December 25th, 1978—her first Christmas without a mother.

The owner, Adam Gessler, stood overseeing the action in jacket and tie. He had gone beyond the concept of the open kitchen by placing cooking stations out in the dining rooms, and then having chefs deliver their own food.

"It's not that important that people see the cooks," Gessler told me, deftly stepping out of the way of an oncoming cart, "but that the cooks see the people. Usually, they're cooking for a wall."

Under his jacket, sweat darkened his shirt. "You can feel the energy," he said enthusiastically, as more chefs-turned-servers barreled past, "of all the people who worked here for the last 150 years." In Warsaw, even restaurants respect the past.

Next door, giving onto Krakowskie Przedmieście, stood another Gessler establishment: Przekąski Zakąski (Snacks & Bites). A curved bar faced a room emptied of tables and overheated with young people. A silver-haired barman—in black vest, white shirt, and black bow tie—poured shots of vodka and handed over dishes of kielbasa and herring. He had an assured, unhurried, almost courtly manner; I watched as he greeted regulars, shaking the men's hands, kissing the women's. There has been a refreshing return to national cuisine: a rash of pierogi restaurants after the obligatory influx of sushi. But this place—open twenty-four hours—managed to do something more: It took Polish standards and made them hip.

~

Friday morning, I sat with Professor Otwinowska in the waiting room of Mokotów Prison. (Now officially named Areszt Śledczy Warszawa-Mokotów.) After a few minutes, the man from the ministry arrived—our liaison—and when I said "Nice to meet you," he replied: "We've already met. I was one of your students. I remember very well. You told a funny story about buying vinegar."

Tomasz led us through the gate, where we relinquished our IDs and cell phones, and into the prison yard. The professor, elegant in her sunhat, clung to my arm as we entered the first building.

Two prisoners were rousted from their cell so we could have a look inside. The professor measured its width by spreading her arms, declaring it bigger than the one she had lived in. And, of course, she had had no TV.

There was the sobering air of any correctional facility, but here it was thickened by the historical echoes. I thought of all the interrogations, hunger strikes, acts of torture, and executions that had taken place within these walls. All the lives lost, the productive years wasted. (A waste that seemed all the more senseless when seen against the prospering normalcy outside.) I thought of all the courageous citizens treated as criminals, the mothers separated from their babies. The babies separated from their mothers.

Our tour ended in the director's office. Bogdan Kornatowski was a tall, handsome, well-built man. He presented each of us with a small etching on glass of the old prison building. He talked with the professor about upcoming events. Then, unexpectedly, he turned his gaze to me.

"What I am about to say may sound a bit strange," he began, then paused, searching for the right words. "Perhaps even ugly. But please tell your wife that she has best wishes from the director of the prison."

The Train to Bagan

The worst train ride of my life may seem an odd illustration of the joy of movement.

It was in the fall of 2012. I had been in Yangon for a week and it felt good to leave my hotel and walk to the train station. Travel suggests motion, and wandering the same streets, returning every night to the same room, constitutes a kind of stasis. You can be in the most incomprehensible city thousands of miles from home and only really feel like a traveler when you board a train, or a bus, to the next one. Movement gives you the nomad's high.

I felt it, strongly, on my Burmese train. And I enjoyed it, thoroughly, for the first hour. Then, as the train picked up speed, things started to deteriorate. I realized that one's enjoyment of movement does not extend to the extreme, at least—I'm thinking of the popularity of roller coasters—not over a period of seventeen hours.

The journey also reminded me that there are times when travel is better in expectation, and more pleasurable in retrospect.

I was the only foreigner on the train to Bagan. I discovered this nineteen hours after boarding, when I stepped onto the pavement of a seemingly deserted station with a handful of Burmese passengers and two rogue taxi drivers by my side.

The duo had appeared in the aisle next to my seat before I'd stood up. I was still in recovery from the worst train ride of my life.

It had started promisingly with a slow glide through the verdant precincts of Yangon. I felt like a passenger on a ride in an amusement park, the only one in the world whose theme was urban life in Southeast Asia. We inched into backyard conversations and sidled up next to open-air kitchens. I gazed out the window captivated, and with that sense of superiority train passengers feel on finding themselves safely removed from the lives they are being granted intimate close-ups of.

So this is why the trip takes so long, I thought. I could live with slow. Thankfully, I had a book with me: *The Old School*, an anthology of essays by W. H. Auden, Antonia White, Anthony Powell, Graham Greene, and others about their schooldays. I had found it in a book stall near my hotel and thought it the perfect companion for a long train journey in a former British colony.

"A good many young women were led to buffoon themselves," I read in Elizabeth Bowen's contribution "The Mulberry Tree." "It seemed fatal not to be at least one thing to excess, and if I could not be outstandingly good at a thing, I preferred to be outstandingly bad at it."

Suddenly, the train started swaying from side to side, making reading difficult. The conductor appeared and pulled my suitcase down from the overhead rack just before it fell on me.

As we gained speed, the swaying was replaced by an even more disconcerting up-and-down motion. I bounced in my seat, often so high that a thick pillow could have been slipped beneath me. The men in *longyi* across the aisle looked much less disturbed, and kept on chatting as if sitting in a tea shop. Living in a country closed off from the world, they had no other experience of trains; for them, being violently shaken was the natural condition of the railway passenger.

The bucking got so bad I seriously worried that the train might derail. It was impossible to read; my book bounced on the window seat in sync with me. I had moved to the aisle seat because the windows were open and the curtains were ferociously flapping in the wind. I looked at my watch and counted the remaining hours: seventeen. I regretted not taking the bus to Bagan.

The chronic jolting made it difficult to drink, let alone eat, which was for the best: I was already dreading the trip to the toilet. Sleep was completely out of the question. This, too, was fortuitous because, as darkness fell and the lights came on, bugs flew in. Every few minutes I had to brush a newly assembled mass of them off my shirt and pants. Most were moths, but some had a more substantial, less benign appearance that I didn't examine closely in my rush to remove them. The window seat became a small insect graveyard.

When I lifted my eyes and took in the entire car—the fluorescent lights, the wildly dancing curtains, the swarming insects, the bobble-head passengers—it seemed to belong to a runaway train in a nightmare. Even the little boy two rows up, who had been all agog at the start of the journey, now wore an aggrieved look.

Also, the air had turned cold—something I hadn't expected. I took a corduroy shirt out of my suitcase and put it on over my long-sleeved shirt, which I had already buttoned at the collar in an effort to keep insects from nesting in my chest hair. I closed my window, but all of the others remained wide open.

I thought of how comfortable the flight home to the States in coach would be.

Eventually, I made the perilous trip to the toilet. Trying to steady myself, I reached like a drunkard for elusive seatbacks. The door to the vestibule had to be unlatched. This was not an easy task, since both of us were moving erratically, and the latch seemed to be at about knee level. Once on the other side, I became the lone target of dive-bombing insects. Here was the real winged creatures' party. The bobbing toilet door presented one more obstacle before the true challenge. Though I wondered if, back in my seat, pants and shoes soaked in urine might repel bugs.

There was no mirror, of course, for economic reasons that were also humane. I had probably never looked so crazed. My extreme discomfort had escalated through the nonstop upheavals into a mild form of madness, a kind of mental *mal de mer* that I hoped would disappear as soon as the journey was over.

Dawn broke and the train slowed down; its nocturnal eruptions ended. I was cold, tired, hungry, rattled, and bug-infested, but, for the first time in many hours, sitting comfortably. Especially after we came to a stop.

Then the two toughs appeared, and asked where I was going. They didn't look like taxi drivers, and their pickup outside carried no markings. Despite my misgivings, they delivered me to my hotel, where I took a hot shower and already began to think warmly of the train that had brought me safely to Bagan and given me a better story than I would have gotten from a TGV.

The Place You Could
Be Looking For

Normally, I don't ask for much in a hotel. It should be reasonably priced (most of my time there is usually spent sleeping), centrally located (ideally, I can walk out the door and be surrounded by street life), and, if possible, it should have some history or character. (Although, I do like to enter luxury hotels and use their restrooms.)

Most hotels are more or less the same, or at least they serve the same function: They are a fundamental, if often very agreeable, part of your trip; they are rarely the star of your trip.

The Atlanta in Bangkok is an exception. More than character, it has a personality, which is a reflection of its owner, one of the most unlikely, and scholarly, hoteliers you'll ever want to meet. (On a return visit in 2012, I was heartened to find that major improvements to the rooms had not altered the endearing, old school essence of the place.) And because it is such a unique hotel, it attracts an interesting clientele. I could easily go to Bangkok—a steamy, fascinating city—and never leave The Atlanta.

"It's not the arrival," they always tell you, "it's the journey that matters." However, sometimes it's neither. Sometimes it's your hotel.

The taxi from the airport eased off the expressway and made a U-turn onto an auxiliary road. It slalomed along the sloping driveway of a darkened high-rise and made a sharp right past a lineup of food stalls—a few were still lit by bare electric bulbs, though it was well past midnight. Finally, we came to a halt at the end of a cul-de-sac in front of a facade of scaffold-like concrete that gave the upper floors a caged look. No sign identified the building; the cabbie seemed as perplexed as I was. Then I noticed the message next to the entrance: SEX TOURISTS NOT WELCOME—and I knew that I had found the right place.

Months earlier, I had asked an acquaintance then living in Thailand if he had any hotel suggestions for Bangkok, and he had immediately recommended The Atlanta. The rooms were Spartan, he warned, but the Art Deco lobby had barely been touched since the opening in 1952, and the restaurant—where Queen Ramphaiphanni had regularly dined—was still excellent. Big band music played in both rooms. The owner, Dr. Charles Henn, was a friend to writers, and displayed books written by guests in the hotel's lobby. Also, he had an aversion to shaking hands.

I had then checked the hotel website. A picture of the lobby—staff stationed behind the arched eyebrows of matching reception desks, a bouqueted roundabout centerpieced in a checkerboard sea—levitated above the words: BANGKOK'S BASTION OF WHOLESOME AND CULTURALLY SENSITIVE TOURISM. LE PATRON MANGE ICI. Not far below ran a line I was soon quoting to friends, neighbors, anyone who asked about my upcoming trip: THE ATLANTA IS UNTOUCHED BY POP CULTURE AND POST-MODERN VULGARITY.

The hotel philosophy on global love for sale was stated farther down: THE ATLANTA IS AGAINST SEX TOURISM. SEX TOURISM IS EXPLOITIVE, SOCIALLY DAMAGING AND CULTURALLY DEMEANING: THOSE WHO WANT TO BUY SEX SHOULD DO SO IN THEIR OWN COUNTRY. This was followed by a condemnation of all illegal activities on hotel premises, concluding with the recommendation: THOSE WHO CANNOT GO ABROAD WITHOUT BEHAVING BADLY SHOULD STAY HOME.

Quietly, I rolled my suitcase into the dimly lit lobby. A thin gray cat lazily licked himself on the roundabout. The night receptionist took my name and asked for payment. I had received a long, single-spaced letter from a Roger Le Phoque, "private secretary to Dr. Charles Henn," confirming my reservation and delineating some of The Atlanta's unorthodoxies, including its policy of accepting neither credit cards nor foreign currencies. However, nothing had been mentioned about payment upon arrival. I had some change from the taxi and three Thai words, *mai pen rai*, meaning, more or less, "not to worry." The receptionist said I could pay in the morning.

Blurrily, I climbed the wraparound staircase, passing on the landing a sign from which the phrase "catamites or prostitutes" jumped out. I had not come across this term for a particular type of boy since reading the opening sentence of Anthony Burgess's 1980 novel *Earthly Powers*: "It was the afternoon of my eighty-first birthday, and I was in bed with my catamite when Ali announced that the archbishop had come to see me." Any hotel that reminds you of literary genius is worth the price.

The price was five hundred baht which, with 7 percent tax, came to approximately $13.70 a night.

~

In the morning, I awoke in a room painted pink and yellow. The air-conditioner hummed reassuringly. Low windows looked out, through the discolored concrete cage, onto the modern apartment house across the street. I took a hot shower with a hand-held nozzle in a curtain-less tub and then, when dressed, went down for breakfast.

The restaurant had the same cool, unperturbed look as the lobby. At the far end was a small annex with books, videos, and the *Times Literary Supplement* on wooden sticks. Waitresses shuffled about in loose-fitting blouses and conservative skirts. Small black-and-white photographs of Siam lined the walls, ceiling fans rotated, baroque music played softly.

An expressionless waitress brought me a menu. The cover read: THE MENU OF THE ATLANTA. PLEASE DO NOT REMOVE. THERE ARE ONLY THREE COPIES OF THIS MENU. I remembered the website had proudly proclaimed this to be "the world's first menu with serious and learned annotations." The first page, however, contained no list of foods, just another pronouncement against prostitutes. Please, I thought, not at breakfast. Still, I took out my notebook. The waitress walked over with a censorious look on her face. I quickly checked to see if I had unthinkingly brought a catamite to dine. Then the waitress told me I was not allowed to write, and looking down at the bottom of the cover I read: COPYRIGHT 2003. NO PART OF THIS MENU MAY BE REPRODUCED.

Properly chastised, I ordered. My pineapple shake arrived on a coaster of The Atlanta. ZERO TOLERANCE & SLEAZE FREE ZONE, it read. NO SEX TOURISTS, JUNKIES, LOUTS & OTHER DEGENERATES.

The reverse side was filled with script:

"There are local expats who walk in with what is obviously a bar-girl. They ignore the sign by the entrance and are oblivious to the ethos of the hotel. They think they can go anywhere and do what they like because they are farangs [foreigners]—they have been spoilt by the tolerant and non-confrontational Thais. Once

here, within these walls, they feel offended if resident guests give them disapproving looks and when the staff do not make them feel welcome. They then pompously say the bargirl is their wife! Courtesy prevents me from asking the unfortunate bargirl what desperation drove her to marry that loser."

—Dr. Henn in conversation with a writer.
Number 5 of an indefinite set.

While eating my pork with pickled radish and rice I thought that, to all the other Atlanta superlatives—"the oldest unaltered hotel foyer in Thailand," "the world's largest selection of Thai vegetarian dishes"—"the world's most didactic hotel" could surely be added. All hotels have rules; this one had a code of ethics. The trendy ones have attitude; The Atlanta had morality. In some ways it reminded me of an English boarding school—the hushed public spaces, the classical music, the books and journals scattered about, the overriding presence of a stern, but wry, headmaster—that for some strange reason served gourmet meals. My breakfast was ambrosial.

I walked outside to see "the first hotel swimming pool" and "the first children's swimming pool" in Thailand, both set in a tropical garden only slightly disturbed by the roar from the neighboring expressway. The resident terrapins, Archibald and Doris, hunkered chastely by their own watering hole.

Back in the lobby, the gray cat had been replaced on the round-about by a brown one. The high glass bookcases contained a good month's worth of well-rounded reading: *A Woman of Bangkok* and *Hvor de ti bud ikke gaelder* (Where the Ten Commandments Don't Matter) kept company with *The Effect of PGE, Gastrin and CCK-8 on Postirradiation Recovery of Small Intestine Epithelium*. P. R. Wiles wrote on the hotel's copy of *The Homology of Glands and Glandularia in the Water Mites*, "Dear Charles, This is the result of some strange ideas I had at The Atlanta after the Seram expedition." E. K. Oppenheimer opined from Myconos (sic):

Alas! Alack!
The N.Y. Times is a hack
Writing a tract
On Bangkok's knack
Blowing their stack
Ending in a cul-de-sac
Leaving The Atlanta no slack.

The scientific papers were right at home, for The Atlanta began life as a laboratory run by Dr. Charles Henn's father, Max. A chemical engineer from Germany, and a world traveler, he came to Bangkok and started The Atlanta Chemical Company, which produced— among other things—dehydrated cobra venom for export to the US. (This according to an article from the local English-language newspaper *The Nation*, now framed in the lobby.) When the business failed, Dr. Henn senior turned the laboratory and offices into a hotel, the snake pit providing the perfect location for the historic pool.

The hotel enjoyed tremendous success. Royalty came to dine and military brass, such as General Westmoreland, stayed as guests. Meanwhile, the scientist turned hotelier became a sort of founding father of Thailand's tourism industry.

However, a slow decline began in the seventies, and by the mid-eighties, it reached a dramatic point. Returning from his studies at Cambridge, the son found the hotel riddled with sex tourists and drug addicts. He set to work on what at any other hostelry would be called "renovation," but at The Atlanta, has to go by the name of "reformation." Not only has the lobby retained its dapper appearance, but the rooms have lingered in the fifties as well (a rude shock to the mini-bar crowd). The alterations were not so much physical (though a good deal of repair work was obviously necessary) and they were certainly not economic (any other hotel would have simply upped the rates to banish the riffraff). Rather, the changes were chiefly behavioral. In what might stand as a unique achievement in the history of hotel management, The Atlanta improved its guest list by preaching decorum.

Framed in the library-museum-lobby was an obituary of Dr. Max Henn, which spoke of his "generosity, old world charm, and incorrigible flirtatiousness—he was a ladies man through and through (and he always had his way without resistance!); he often admitted that that was his only vice (he had no other; indeed he was never a night-lifer, never went night-clubbing, never went to the bars).

"[He] tirelessly instilled in his nearest and dearest an endless dedication to learning and competence, an impatience with weakness, a loathing for stupidity and for those who would work without engaging their brains."

His portrait hung on one wall; a youthful portrait of Charles's mother, a beautiful Thai, graced another. A footnoted guide to Thai culture and customs, written by the son as a service to guests, sat atop a lectern, while the son's books—*The History of Materialism, L'Idée de l'État*—filled the glass bookcase above the two roll-top desks in the small space labeled "Guests' Writing Room." (While running The Atlanta, Charles—once again distinguishing himself in the hotel management community—taught for nearly two decades at the Graduate School of Political Science and International Studies at the University of Buckingham in England.) Tucked away in a corner sat a pair of computer terminals.

Heading up to my room, I stopped and read more fully about prostitutes and catamites. (A guest could spend an entire day reading at The Atlanta without ever opening a book.) They were, of course, persona non grata. HOWEVER, the sign instructed, A GUEST WHO GETS DESPERATE AND FINDS IT NECESSARY TO BRING BACK A BARGIRL OR THE

LIKE MIGHT BE TOLERATED PROVIDED NO LAW IS BROKEN. NOTE THE WORD IS TOLERATED, NOT WELCOME. DON'T EXPECT US OR FELLOW GUESTS TO BE POLITE ABOUT IT. WE WILL NOT APOLOGIZE FOR BEING UNWELCOMING, RUDE, OR DOWNRIGHT OFFENSIVE.

After less than a day at The Atlanta, I was seized by two conflicting desires: to bring back a bargirl and to meet Charles Henn.

~

All hotels are surrogates for home; some of them are more luxurious, some of them less. Even the lowly ones we cherish, because in a place where all our senses are stretched—a new city, a foreign land—they make it okay to fall unconscious. They conquer the alien with the intimacy of a bed. Staying in a hotel is as close as we get to returning to the womb.

This is why you often see people deliberating in the lobby, back-slapping in the bar, opening their doors to room-service carts. They're in no hurry to brave the elements. Here is safety and order; out there the big, thrumming unknown.

The Atlanta offered no bar (a magnet for bargirls) or room service, but it had a comfortable, clubby feel that made it an especially difficult place to leave. Stepping out in the morning, even into the vibrant pageant that is Bangkok, I always had the nagging suspicion that I was going to miss something good. When I returned in the evening, the people huddled in the restaurant somehow looked more intriguing than the in-house diners at other hotels.

Breakfast was a much-anticipated event. My second morning, I studied the menu while listening to madrigals. In addition to footnotes, giving the historical and cultural backgrounds of the various dishes, were literary quotations. "There is no love sincerer than the love of food."—George Bernard Shaw. (One that, banned from writing in my notebook, I committed to memory.) In the back of the menu, there were specials named for friends of The Atlanta.

When my banana shake arrived, I eagerly picked it up and turned over the coaster.

"There are only two things to do with prospective guests: welcome them if they are decent and clean, or welcome somebody else if they are not. We don't rent rooms to Calibans."

—*Dr. Henn's instruction to reception.*
Number 3 of an indefinite set.

"What does yours say?" I asked the woman at the neighboring table.
"What?"
"What's written on the other side of your coaster?"
"I didn't know anything was."
She was a freelance writer from New York City, traveling around Asia on a quest for self-realization. Perhaps this explained her blissful unawareness of her immediate surroundings. Though, she was very conscious of her pocketbook. "You can get better rooms at this price in other parts of the city," she said. "I don't like the Sukhumvit area."

The Atlanta, never at a loss for words, had a sign at the reception desk for people like her. COMPLAINTS ARE NOT PERMITTED, it read, NOT AT THE PRICES WE CHARGE.

The hotel sat next to a Baptist church at the end of Sukhumvit Soi 2, one of the quietest of the numerous dead-end streets that stretch off from Sukhumvit Road like the elongated legs of a centipede. Sukhumvit Soi 4, by contrast, throbbed with bars—musical stock-yards—that spilled forth women of wide-ranging affections. It was one of those places in Bangkok where Western men suffering from low self-esteem can receive instant cures.

The night I discovered it, Charles's exhortations no longer seemed so excessive. Nor did they derive, I realized, from simply a moral position. For over half a century, his family's hotel had graced a neighborhood that he had watched turn from modest to grotesque.

The sex industry had become a blight on his home, its leech-like culture an affront to his sensibilities. In one of the articles displayed in the lobby, he was quoted as saying: "I am more in sympathy with the 19th century, or pre-war Europe, than I am with post-war Europe, let alone the 21st century." This sensibility was reflected in his inheritance. Hotels by their very nature transport you to a different place; The Atlanta deposited you in another time. That it was a little voluble in doing so was understandable; it was a strident fogey because the world outside had become a strident boor. It didn't just provide a wholesome environment for foreign tourists, it carved a preserve of civility out of the encroaching 'tude. It was as advertised—"untouched by pop culture and post-modern vulgarity."

Returning to the hotel that night I noticed a sign (what else?) above the entrance: THIS IS THE PLACE YOU'RE LOOKING FOR—IF YOU KNOW IT. IF YOU DON'T, YOU'LL NEVER FIND IT. Finally, I saw the hotel's name. It was engraved on a small silver plaque by the door.

~

"I wouldn't think this is the sort of place Americans would like."

My new breakfast neighbors were two cheerful, stereotyping Englishwomen on vacation. (Though, perhaps they had met the writer from New York.)

"I rather like that the staff's not friendly," the brunette said, smiling. "We were in the lobby yesterday and a woman came in, without a reservation, and asked if she could see a room. And the receptionist said, 'No.' 'Well, can I have a brochure?' 'No.'" Surely, I thought, a Caliban.

After they had gone, I picked up the list of hotel videos. The introduction, which took up three pages, explained that guests would find no pornography (even though, as was pointedly noted, it is available in some upscale hotels), no gratuitous violence, and no pop music videos because they "are common and can be found elsewhere." Awaiting their viewing pleasure instead were numerous films set in Asia (an aside remarked on the large number of Western movie stars who've appeared in such pictures, and a long list followed with all of their names) as well as great films built around the theme of food, including *Tampopo*, *Eat Drink Man Woman*, *Babette's Feast*, and *Big Night*. *La Grande Bouffe* was not in the collection because, for one thing, its humor was scatological.

My pineapple shake arrived on its aphoristic coaster.

"The staff are nice; I am not—which is why the staff are nice. Anyone who expects me to be an obliging, hand-wringing sort of inn-keeper will be sorely disappointed."

—Dr. Henn in conversation. Number 1 of an indefinite set.

~

On my next-to-last morning at The Atlanta, a young woman sat down at the table next to mine and then asked the waitress if she could take breakfast in the garden.

"I could not stand the music," she explained when I found her, a half hour later, sipping tea in the shade.

"You don't like baroque?" I asked.

"I think this morning I could not have standed any music."

Jutta was a scientist from Germany (like Max Henn), but her specialty was nutrition. She was doing research in Bangkok before heading back to "her" village in Laos to gather more data for her doctoral thesis. She wondered if I had met Charles.

I said I hadn't even seen him, though I felt as if I knew him.

She told me that he was setting up a patronage that would allow people in the arts and sciences to stay at the hotel for extended periods. "He wants to encourage people to meet and talk," she said, "like we're doing here."

All over the world I have visited famous literary hotels—the Ritz in Paris, Raffles in Singapore—that today have rates prohibitive to any author not on the bestseller list. The Atlanta, in yet another cap feather, was a writers' hotel that writers could actually afford.

Jutta said that Charles had planted a vine that is reputed to prevent as well as treat malaria, and together we searched the garden for it. *Tinospora crispa* was its Latin name, she said, *kheua kha hor* in Lao. The Laotian woman from the hotel travel office joined us in the hunt, leading us outside and into the parking lot of the Baptist church. A young man appeared from the parish hall and, speaking with the two women, said that the vine we were interested in was available at the market. He'd bring it to the hotel at six that evening.

"That's what I like here," Jutta said. "You ask for something and one thing leads to another. People help you. They look after you."

At precisely six o'clock the man appeared outside the hotel on his bicycle, a plastic shopping bag of *tinospora crispa* hanging from the handlebars. Jutta was nowhere to be seen. The punctual Thai and the tardy German. I handed him five hundred baht (the price of a one-night stay) and carried the knobby vine up to my room.

The next day I gave Jutta her medicine, put in a request at the reception desk to see Charles Henn, packed my suitcase, and then ate lunch—a delicious Vegetarian Mussulman Curry—to the sounds of regal jazz. A sign outside the restaurant carried the schedule: 12 NOON TO 1 P.M.—MUSIC COMPOSED BY HM THE KING OF THAILAND IS PLAYED DURING THIS TIME EVERY DAY. MUSIC FROM 5 P.M. MONDAYS & FRIDAYS—BIG BAND, HISTORIC RECORDINGS. TUESDAYS, THURSDAYS & SATURDAYS—CLASSIC JAZZ. WEDNESDAYS & SUNDAYS—BIG BAND, MODERN RECORDINGS. MUSIC SELECTION BY CHARLES HENN. ALL ROYALTIES PAID.

After my meal, I retired to the garden to pass the time before heading to the station. As I was writing my notes, a man appeared in white slacks (I was sitting down) and a dark green shirt (the button-down collar cavalierly—or professorially—left unbuttoned). He introduced himself as Charles Henn.

This was a surprise. He shied away from publicity, to such an extent that he had acquired a reputation as a mysterious figure. He didn't look at all as I had pictured him: wizened and sour; instead he was boyish, almost jaunty, with something of a mischievous twinkle in his eyes. A wave of relief washed over me, but I didn't offer my hand.

We moved into the restaurant, where I told him that in three decades of travel I had never come across a hotel like his.

"This is largely because I am not a hotel man," he said. "I am an academic. My intellectual love is political theory." He added, "I don't have the heart to sell it. It is the one concrete thing my parents made. The satisfaction comes from the fact that I've kept it going. And that guests love it so much."

It was not a profitable venture, he told me, and was not meant to be. "I don't even know what the rooms cost. My mother takes care of the financial side."

His concern was its spirit—its appearance and character. He insisted that the decor, at least in the common areas, conform as closely as possible to his father's original design.

The staff provided a measure of continuity, with families staying on sometimes for generations. "It's almost like a tenured job," he said. "The staff know what to do but, being Thai, they often don't do it. But the loyalty is there. They don't have the superficial manners that you find in some other hotels, but they have a tremendous sense of goodwill toward the guests.

"Security is good here because the staff feel it's home. Nothing ever goes missing; it wouldn't occur to them to take something."

I asked about the signs and messages. They appeared after his father's death in 2002. "Bangkok is viewed as a place where you can do anything," he said with the faint hint of a twinkle, clearly relishing the fact that he had created within it a tasteful space where you can't.

As he talked, it became clear that he was not the puritan the signage might suggest. He had become, he said proudly, the first non-British member of the British Academy of Gastronomes. He expressed surprising sympathy, considering all his dictums, for older men who come to Bangkok for obvious reasons. "Often they're widowers or divorced. They treat the girls much better than the young ones do. The young ones say, 'We're not sex tourists, not like those guys with their beer guts.' I say, 'You just hope that at that age your gut is not so big and that you still have a libido to want a girl.' I don't condone them. I just prefer them to the young ones."

I complimented him on the music. "Truthfully," he said, "I tolerate jazz. I like opera, and classical music. I don't listen to modern composers."

He was a patron of the traditional performing arts, and was currently working with a theater that was putting on a production of a scene from the *Ramakien*, the Thai version of the Hindu epic, *Ramayana*.

"I'm translating the libretto so that they can have subtitles in English," he explained. "I translate from classical Thai into Shakespearean English." I thought of the father's obituary, and his antipathy "for those who would work without engaging their brains."

A young woman had come in during our conversation and taken a seat at the far end of the restaurant. Charles now told me that she was from the theater, here for their appointment. I thanked him for his time, and apologized for taking so much of it. Then I walked out to the lobby to collect my bags while the hotelier moved on to his libretto.

What I Like About Key West

I first went to Key West in 1991 to write about its Literary Seminar. The town's attractiveness to writers—from Ernest Hemingway to Joy Williams—was unusual (one didn't automatically associate the literary with Florida) but well-known. I expected, when not attending panels of famous writers, to visit Papa's old house—perhaps the city's most popular attraction. Key West, as everyone knew, had become a tourist town.

So I was pleasantly surprised when I got off Duval Street and discovered a neighborly place of porches and alleys, one that recalled—in its components if not its colors—towns I'd known growing up in the Northeast. No one had told me that Key West would resemble Mechanicsburg, PA.

On that first visit I stayed at the Pier House, at the busy end of Duval, and detected in my chambermaid a familiar accent. Jolanta was from Poland, part of the first wave of Poles that descended on Key West at the end of the Cold War to work in the shops, hotels, restaurants, and bars. They were eventually joined by Russians and other Eastern Europeans who today add still another new note—a touch of the Slavic—to one's visit to the Conch Republic.

For many people, a visit to Key West is a trip to the fringe—a louche dead end filled with exotic slackers. "If there was any place on the map of the United States where the elevated ideology of being an American finally unraveled," Jonathan Raban wrote in *Hunting Mister Heartbreak*, "it was on the Keys."

Yet, if you live elsewhere in Florida—and happen to have grown up in another state—Key West provides a nostalgic return to normalcy.

The first time I drove into town, from my new home in Fort Lauderdale, I was struck not by the alien but by the once-familiar: porches, alleys, chickens, white picket fences, people on bicycles. I had left the world of condos and gated communities and seemed to be on a childhood trip to grandmother's house, a house that—in a bewildering but beguiling twist—had been uprooted from central Pennsylvania and set down in a tropical garden.

Turning onto Duval, I headed down the Conch version of Main Street USA. As at Disney World, the buildings were pretty, and built, it seemed somehow, on a slightly smaller scale. (The Cuban influence?) There were numerous places to buy ice cream. Mixed in with them, of course, were loudmouth bars and window displays of X-rated T-shirts. Purists constantly bemoan the scourge of T-shirt shops, yet this item of clothing is single-handedly keeping the aphorist alive.

Key West has long been a writers' town. The purpose of that first trip was to report on the annual Key West Literary Seminar, which that year (1991) was devoted to travel writing. The keynote speaker, John Malcolm Brinnin, was also a resident, and he validated my impressions of the place by noting that he and his septuagenarian friends lived very much as they had as children: They wore short pants, they rode around on bikes, they took afternoon naps. This constituted more of a regression than an unraveling. Though his talk, "Travel and the Sense of Wonder," reached such heights of sage eloquence that it was published a year later by the Library of Congress.

My room was at the Pier House and my chambermaid was Polish. This seemed serendipitous until I discovered that the town was sprinkled with Poles. They made beds, bused tables, washed dishes, poured drinks, and scooped ice cream (often after a stint in Chicago). I found myself, remarkably, in an evocative old-fashioned town covering a conference of writers I admired while in my spare time brushing up on my Polish. Adding to my satisfaction with the world was the fact that it was January and I didn't need a coat.

Subsequent trips to Key West happily reinforced for me this unlikely triumvirate—for a wayward, subtropical isle—of the bygone, the literary, and the Polish.

The literary seminar didn't tackle travel writing again until 2005, a gap that might conceivably be attributed to the fact that the town has inspired so much bad travel writing. This time I stayed, more appropriately, in a three-story Victorian with a porch *and* a balcony. Every morning I'd come downstairs and find Dervla Murphy, the intrepid Irish travel writer, eating breakfast in the garden. I drank tea with Pico Iyer at an outdoor café. One night I went barhopping with a former poet laureate.

When not attending panels, I researched a story about the Eastern European workforce. I was the travel editor of the newspaper in Fort Lauderdale at the time and, while I'd read hundreds of articles on Key West, I'd never come across anything about the heavily accented and sometimes highly educated help. They were service people, invisible to anyone not transported by the accent.

As I did my legwork, I discovered that over the years the Poles had been joined by others from the old neighborhood: Russians, Hungarians, Ukrainians, Moldovans, Belarusians, Lithuanians, Latvians, Czechs, who now outnumbered the Poles. As if an indication of this, my chambermaid this time hailed from Prague.

A local historian told me that, in the early nineties, Casa Marina was the first hotel to start hiring Poles. Most people I talked to spoke very highly of their Czech carpenter or their Latvian salesgirls. I met a Belarusian waitress—a former English major—whose favorite American writer was O. Henry. A young Polish woman, working in a sunglasses shop, wrote poems in her free time that she described as "hermetic." I was thrilled by the meeting of the literary and the Slavic.

~

A few years later, I returned to Key West to write an article about Casa Marina. I had missed it on my first visit, since it's not in the center of town but tucked away—if a grand hotel can ever be "tucked"—in a quiet neighborhood bordering the Atlantic. Envisioned by Henry Flagler, the father of modern Florida, and constructed in 1920, it seems less a part of Key West than of the Florida tradition of great outpost hotels. Because tourists were—at least in the southern half of the state—the real pioneers, hotels are our most historic and iconic structures. They are to Florida what castles are to Europe.

When I mentioned to a friend that I would be writing about the hotel, he promptly informed me that the bar had been the setting for a fistfight between Ernest Hemingway and Wallace Stevens. This was not true, I discovered after doing a little research; the fight took place on a street in town. But the hotel was where Stevens would stay when he'd come seeking relief from Connecticut winters. Most of the letters in the last chapter of *The Contemplated Spouse: The Letters of Wallace Stevens to Elsie* were written on Casa Marina stationery. One informed the left-behind partner: "Robert Frost was on the beach this morning and is coming to dinner this evening. We are having what is called conk [sic] chowder, a thing in which he is interested."

Stevens was more impressed with the hotel than he was with the town. "The delightful porches full of palms on which you take your meals are just as good as they ever were," he wrote to his wife in

1935, a year after proclaiming: "Key West is extremely old-fashioned and primitive. The movie theatres are little bits of things." Though it inspired "The Idea of Order at Key West," if not also "The Emperor of Ice-Cream."

Al fresco dining at Casa Marina has since moved from the porches to the small beach, where every evening, weather permitting, white-clothed tables are set up in the sand. Inside the hotel, the bar in which the famous fight never happened is decorated with enlarged, black-and-white photographs: Henry Flagler on the day his train first pulled into town; a shirtless Harry Truman proudly holding up a fish; John F. Kennedy sitting in the backseat of a convertible and getting an earful from a local in swim trunks. There is a picture of Tennessee Williams having drinks with Truman Capote but, sadly, none of Wallace Stevens sipping soup with Robert Frost.

Leaving the hotel and taking a stroll, I was reminded that the town's homey otherness is heightened at night. The humid air is perfumed with flowers and salt. Softly lit rooms endowed with antiques appear through cracks in front-yard jungles. Porch lights produce primeval shadows. The susurrations of palms—or are they Poles?—caress the ear.

My Days with the Anti-Mafia

For years I had been hearing about a group in Sicily that was fighting back against the Mafia. In the spring of 2010 I did an Internet search, which brought up a number of news stories, most of them from British publications. While providing me with good background information, they also convinced me that the movement was deserving of more in-depth treatment.

I found the website of the anti-Mafia organization Addiopizzo, and contacted the man who headed its tourism division. I arrived in Palermo a few months later.

My bed-and-breakfast was run by a woman who was a member of Addiopizzo. I visited the office of the man I had contacted, who gave me the brief history of the organization and his involvement with it. Then, with a group of Italian tourists from the mainland, we went on an anti-Mafia tour of Palermo.

Over the course of the week I talked to a variety of people—a writer, a policeman, a priest—who enlightened me about life in Sicily. I visited one of the country's worst slums. One day I ate an al fresco lunch with a restaurateur who is hated by the Mafia and watched as a Mafioso walked past our table. At that moment, my education stopped being safe and hypothetical and became disconcertingly, dramatically real.

Postscript: Addiopizzo has grown from 460 members in 2010 to over 1,000 today.

She sat reading in the garden of Monreale Cathedral, dwarfed by an ancient, leathery banyan. Except for the book, she fit the popular image of the young Siciliana: black hair, black dress, black shoes. She looked as if she'd come from Mass. I took a seat at the other end of the bench, from where I could make out the title of her book: *The Portrait of a Lady.*

"That's a good book," I said.

"*Scusi?*" she asked, startled by my intrusion.

"Henry James is a wonderful writer," I said.

She smiled without looking at me.

"I'm trying to improve my English," she explained.

Her name was Rosalina. She had recently returned from Milan to look after her ailing mother in Palermo. "A lot of young people leave Sicily," she said. Her brother lived in Milan.

"We are not good citizens," she said bluntly. "Do you know what I mean?"

I mentioned the litter, which, after only two days, had made an impression.

"Yes. We live in a kind of paradise. We have the sun and the sea. We think everything will take care of itself."

I told her that I had come to write about the anti-Mafia organization Addiopizzo.

"I think a lot of people don't understand the importance of this organization," she said.

"Perhaps the new generation will," I suggested.

She looked unconvinced. "People were more active in the eighties," she said.

~

My bed & breakfast sat at the end of a quiet street not far from the port. (I had arrived on a cruise ship Friday evening and had stayed on board for the weekend excursions, the last of which was to Monreale.) There was no sign outside the building, just the name SOLELUNA among the list of tenants by the door. I took the elevator to the third floor and rang the bell on the right. The door opened to reveal a woman in big round glasses topped by a tousle of salt-and-pepper hair. "I am Patrizia," she said, pretty much exhausting her English if not her warm welcome. Then she showed me to my room, where two single beds sat a little forlornly under a high ceiling.

Going out to explore, I found Palermo in a deep sleep. It was mid-afternoon on a Sunday in mid-August. Streets narrowed and darkened, at one point opening up to a sunlit intersection of stupendous decay. Abandoned buildings, sick with graffiti and boarded-up windows, seemed in competition to see which one could hold up the longest. I had read that some bombed-out neighborhoods had never been fixed up after World War II; that Sicily was perennially ignored by Rome. But stumbling upon a decades-old dereliction—after two days of churches and palaces—was deeply alarming. This looked like Havana, not a major city of the European Union.

I crossed Via Vittorio Emanuele and plunged into another maze. A clutter of balconies blackened the airspace until I emerged into a small square mushroomed with café umbrellas. An aproned waiter stepped from a door beneath the letters: ANTICA FOCACCERIA S. FRANCESCO. I knew the place from photographs, though they had always shown armed guards stationed in front—placed there because the owner had not only refused to pay protection money, he had gone to court and identified his extortionist. I put their absence down to the dormancy of August.

Via Merlo led to Piazza Marina, where the shuttered windows of old *palazzi* gazed down on the dusty Giardino Garibaldi—its fence a rusting riot of nautical themes. It struck me as possibly the psy-chological heart of the city, the place where people would gather if there were people. Admiring one of the garden's banyans, I came to a plaque:

IN QUESTO LUOGO IL 12 MARZO 1909 ALLE ORE 20:45
PER PRODITORIA MANO MAFIOSA TACQUE LA VITA DI
JOE PETROSINO
LIEUTENANT DELLA POLIZIA DI NEW YORK
LA CITTÀ RICORDA ED ONORA IL SACRIFICIO DELL'
INVESTIGATORE ITALO-AMERICANO

(IN THIS PLACE ON MARCH 12, 1909, AT 8:45 PM
THE HAND OF THE MAFIA SILENCED THE LIFE OF
JOE PETROSINO
NEW YORK POLICE LIEUTENANT
THE CITY RECORDS AND HONORS THE SACRIFICE
OF THIS ITALIAN-AMERICAN INVESTIGATOR)

Not far away, an inscription on a wall—in Italian and German—identified the house as a place where Johann Wolfgang von Goethe had stayed while on his visit to Palermo in 1787. It noted that his subsequent book, *Italian Journey*, had called Sicily the key to understanding Italy.

A little to the east, Piazza Kalsa breathed some life. Two boys rode one bicycle back and forth, and a father pulled down the pants of his son so he could urinate into the bushes. Smoke from grills wafted over from surrounding streets. Next to the Church of Santa Teresa, a large hand-painted cart held a statue of the Virgin. The floor of the cart was covered on two sides with artificial roses, while the center sparkled with shards of broken glass. It seemed an odd decorative touch, but perhaps it doubled as a glittery, have-no-mercy message to thieves.

~

My first breakfast at SoleLuna was eaten in the company of two young women from Genoa. They had come to the B&B, they said, on the recommendation of a friend. They hadn't realized that it was owned by a member of Addiopizzo—the organization that gives support to businesses that refuse to pay protection money (*pizzo*) to the Mafia. They were accidental ethical tourists.

Patrizia joined us, and I asked Francesca to ask her about her membership in Addiopizzo. Patrizia said that she had never been asked to pay the pizzo; that she joined the organization out of a sense of solidarity. (The full name of her lodging is SoleLuna della Solidarietà Bed & Breakfast.) I asked if she was afraid.

"No, no, no," she said dismissively, after hearing the translation. "No problem," she said, waving her hands and shaking her mop of salt-and-pepper hair.

Addiopizzo was born in 2004, when a few recent university graduates considered opening a bar in Palermo. Of course this would entail, as someone pointed out to them, paying protection money. (At the time, the Mafia extorted an estimated $200 million annually from Palermo businesses, with rates that ranged from about $300 for a bar to as much as $1,500 for a large hotel.) The young men, instead of starting their new business, went out late at night and blitzed the city with stickers carrying a message that translated to: "An entire people that pays the pizzo is a people without dignity."

It was a courageous act. In 1991 Libero Grassi, a clothing manufacturer, sent an open letter to the *Giornale di Sicilia* that began: "Dear Extortionist"; nine months after it was published, he was killed. Other people who had stood up to the Mafia had had their factories torched, their stores ransacked, their pets killed. The retaliation of the so-called "Honored Society" is a well-documented, and unhealthily glorified, phenomenon.

However, support for Addiopizzo grew, so much that by 2010 it had over 460 members—everything from the Accademia Siciliana Shiatsu to the Zsa Zsa Monamour dance club—that refused to pay protection money. (Though considering all the businesses in Palermo, this was still a modest number. And skeptics say that many of the people who claim they don't pay the pizzo actually do.) There is a store on Via Vittorio Emanuele that sells only products made by pizzo-free enterprises. Comitato Addiopizzo has a comprehensive website, giving information in most EU languages (including Finnish and Lithuanian), and it even has a travel arm, which offers anti-Mafia tours. I was signed up for one on Tuesday.

Today, however, I needed to go shopping, as I hadn't seen my suitcase since check-in in Miami. After breakfast, I left SoleLuna and walked the length of Via Roma, stopping in every men's store I passed. As disheartening as the merchandise—shirts defaced with logos, zippers, bogus coats of arms, meaningless scraps of English—was the reception from the shop assistants. It wasn't a surprise, though. In *The Honoured Society: The Sicilian Mafia Observed*, Norman Lewis wrote: "By comparison with the Italy of Rome—above all of Naples—Sicily is morose and withdrawn." The British travel writer developed a great affection for the place but noted in a later book, *In Sicily*, that he rarely heard the sound of laughter.

The shop assistants along Via Roma—and later Via Maqueda—lived up to the stereotype. Granted, it was a stifling week in August when anyone still working had a right to be irritable and pining for the beach. But most places I went in Palermo—cafes, newsstands, gelaterias—I was met with an impassive, unchanging expression. It seemed the facial posture of a people who had long ago learned to be suspicious of strangers, initially those who arrived from other lands, and now those who appeared from outside a protective, vetted circle.

In every store, I wondered if the owner paid the pizzo.

~

The bus traveled north along Via della Libertà and dropped me on a wide boulevard lined with large apartment houses. Heading toward the entrance of one, I saw a handsome young man dressed in a T-shirt and shorts. He introduced himself as Edoardo Zaffuto—the man I'd been corresponding with by email. The T-shirt, I now noticed, carried an anti-pizzo message.

I followed Edoardo up to his office on the second floor. The previous tenant, he told me, had been a Mafioso. A cutout of a tree occupied one corner, with headshots of men—Libero Grassi, Giovanni Falcone, Paolo Borsellino (the two anti-Mafia magistrates assassinated in 1992)—pasted on its branches. Above them arched the words, in Italian: "You are not alone anymore."

Edoardo gave me a booklet of Addiopizzo businesses, and a large city map with their locations—as well as that of his office—clearly marked. Then, taking a seat, he told me his story.

In 2004, he had been working at a small publishing company with one of the originators of the sticker campaign. He asked if he could join them. They would go out once a week, often as late as two a.m.; some wore hoods to hide their identities.

"We were scared," Edoardo admitted. "We were not sure what we could risk."

After spreading their message through stickers and the Internet (methods ancient and modern), they started to recruit businesses. "It was hard," Edoardo said, "to ask shopkeepers to join a pizzo-free organization." So they began with businesses that had never paid the pizzo, or whose family members had been Mafia victims. After two years, Addiopizzo had a hundred members.

They also recruited consumers. Edoardo got up to show me another wall hanging—a framed page from the *Giornale di Sicilia*. It contained a list of names of "normal citizens"—3,500 of them—who were committed to shopping at pizzo-free establishments (and—even more impressively—unopposed to having this fact reported in the newspaper). It was a striking testament to the courage of the common Sicilian, and it seemed to refute what Rosalina had said.

Edoardo stressed that Addiopizzo was not running a boycotting campaign. "We don't want to accuse those who pay the pizzo," he said. "Most of them are victims. And they are scared."

People who have refused the Mafia have paid the price. Having armed guards outside your restaurant, for instance, is not exactly a boon to business. One man with a paint and hardware store saw his warehouse destroyed by fire. "In the last years," Edoardo said, "the Mafia prefers not to kill people. But destroying this man's business was like killing him."

But it didn't work. Addiopizzo gave him assistance, as did a lot of those "normal citizens" who collected money for his employees. Usually, Edoardo noted, employees flee a company that's been attacked by the Mafia.

The government provided the man with another warehouse, and the boss who had ordered the fire, as well as the henchman who had set it, were both arrested. "It was a critical moment," Edoardo said. "Otherwise, Addiopizzo would have appeared weaker than the Mafia. It demonstrated that the city was changed, and that people were ready to stand up to the Mafia."

Our chat was interrupted by the arrival of the tour group. They entered the room and took seats in a circle, then Edoardo gave them an extensive briefing. He spoke more fluently than in English, but with the same quiet intensity. When he finished, he asked everyone to say something about themselves. There were two middle-aged women from Rome, a couple from Milan traveling with their teenage son, a twenty-something couple from Verona, three young women from Veneto, and a vintner from central Italy—Beatrice—who sat next to me and occasionally translated. Even when a bottle of wine was opened, and some cookies passed around, the assembly had more the air of a mission than of a holiday.

We were too numerous to all fit in the van, so I joined the women from Veneto in their rental car. We drove down residential streets and parked in front of a ten-story apartment house. A small olive tree stood in front, its branches dripping with caps, ribbons, and an Italian flag. Here, Edoardo explained, Paolo Borsellino was killed by a car bomb, along with his bodyguards. He had just come from paying a visit to his mother, who lived in the building. The filial circumstances of his death made it somehow even more repugnant.

Stuffed animals and scrawled messages still sanctified the site. NOT ALL SICILIANS ARE MAFIA, read one note, AND NOT ALL MAFIA ARE SICILIAN. Another carried the words: "THE FIGHT AGAINST THE MAFIA SHOULD BE A CULTURAL AND MORAL MOVEMENT THAT INVOLVES EVERYONE, ESPECIALLY THE YOUNG GENERATION."—PAOLO BORSELLINO.

Back in our vehicles, we headed out of the city and up Mount Pellegrino to the Santa Rosalia Sanctuary. "Because the Mafia," Beatrice had said to me, in a voice heavy with exasperation at the irony, "are very Catholic." The patron saint of Palermo, Rosalia is credited with saving the city from the plague in 1624.

A yellow convent rose out of rock at the top of a long series of steps. "In 2005," Edoardo said, as we climbed upwards, "Addiopizzo put a sign on the sanctuary that read: SANTA ROSALIA—FREE US FROM THE PIZZO. She freed us from the plague," he explained. "Now the plague is the Mafia."

Inside the chapel, everyday crowds jostled their way past celestial objects. The loaded spectacle of commotion and reverence—common to any pilgrimage site—was amplified by the fact that the sanctuary was contained in a cave fourteen hundred feet high. The devout and the curious made their way through the dank cavity to a statue of Rosalia, backlit in blue. Leaving, I noticed high on a wall in the vestibule a plaque commemorating the visit of Goethe, who, it noted, had "contemplated the primitive simplicity of the sanctuary," and the devotion of the people. Not much had changed in the ensuing two centuries.

"It's important for Addiopizzo to relate to the Church," Edoardo said when we got outside, "because it still has a lot of influence on people." In the past, the Church was indifferent to—even accepting of—the Mafia, but that was changing. "After the murder of Giovanni Falcone," Edoardo said, "Pope John Paul II spoke out against the Mafia." (A rare papal condemnation of the organization that came, perhaps not coincidentally, from the first non-Italian pope since the sixteenth century.) In 1993, the Mafia killed a priest, Father Giuseppe "Pino" Puglisi, who worked in a poor neighborhood of Palermo. "He tried to organize free-time activities for kids," Edoardo said, who might otherwise have gone to the Mafia.

Back in the car, Agnese apologized for her English, which was infinitely better than my unexcused Italian. "Problem in Italy," she said. "People only speak Italian."

"Yes," I said. "Outside of Italy, Italian's not really spoken much."

"Only Formula 1," she said. "And opera."

We came down from the mountain and were soon driving along a street sprinkled with beachgoers and lined with villas. This was Mondello—Palermo's resort town. We found the rest of the group on the seaside promenade, in front of an impressive Art Nouveau bathhouse.

As we strolled, I asked Maria where she lived in Rome. "Near St. Peter's," she said, before telling me that she had been baptized in the basilica. "My father worked at the Vatican," she explained. "He wasn't a priest," she said smiling. "He was an architect."

We came to the door of the Renato Bar. Among its many decals was one identifying the place as pizzo-free. "At first they didn't want to put it," Edoardo said. "But after they did, they saw that more people came."

We pulled a few of the outdoor tables together and they soon filled with bowls of gelato, plates of brioche, and tulip glasses of *granita* (the delicious flavored ice that is a specialty of Sicily). A late afternoon snack (right about the time I'm usually thinking about dinner). The young man from Verona insisted I take some of his brioche and dip it into my almond *granita*; I did, blissfully putting sweet on sweet. I learned that the group was spending the entire week on an Addiopizzo tour. They were even staying at a pizzo-free hotel on the beach. (Very few hotels are members of Addiopizzo; when I asked Edoardo the reason, he suggested that it's perhaps because they've been paying the pizzo longer than most businesses.)

Getting up to leave, we looked across the beach toward Mount Pellegrino which, from this side, resembled a bloodhound in repose.

~

The next day, I picked up my new trousers (which needed to be shortened), put on my new shirt (its blue stripes partially disguising the logo), and walked out of the SoleLuna feeling like a Palermitano—a sensation that only strengthened when I bought a bouquet. But I still wanted my suitcase back.

Stefania lived in a modern building on a quiet street a few blocks west of the designer shops on Via della Libertà. She was a writer, a friend of a friend. Her apartment was on the top floor, and when she opened the door her daughter's new puppy aimed enthusiastically for my white pants.

The daughter was studying anthropology in Turin; the son, philosophy in Berlin. The far-flung children of Sicilian intelligentsia. The University of Palermo, the son said, had some good professors, but "the worst administration in Italy."

A friend by the name of Maruzza arrived, and we moved to the table.

"I hope you like pasta," Stefania said, passing me a bowl of fusilli cooked with eggplant and tomatoes. This was followed by cold plates: meatballs, pecorino cheese, slices of potato, more eggplant and tomatoes. The daughter opened a bottle of wine, and then placed it on the table, where it sat untouched. (Was it the guest's duty to pour in Sicily? Nothing I'd read had indicated as such.)

Maruzza did most of the talking, telling us all about her bags. It was a bit of a sore subject with me, though hers were handbags made by women in the worst slum in Palermo—a place with the unlikely name of ZEN 2. (There was also a ZEN 1, I was told, the name an acronym for Zona Espansione Nord, or Northern Expansion Zone.)

"It is the Bronx of Palermo," someone said.

"The police won't go there," someone else added. "Everyone there is Mafia."

I said I'd like to see it.

Stefania got up and unwrapped a box that Maruzza had brought. It contained not pastries, but exquisite miniature ice cream cones—each tiny individual scoop encased in a protective dark chocolate shell.

When they were consumed, Stefania showed me the apartment: the wrap-around balcony, with a distant view of the sea; her office off the living room, the walls lined with books. Still, she spent quite a bit of time on the mainland. "It is hard to live here," she said, foregoing an explanation while looking out the window.

~

Maruzza picked me up near the SoleLuna the following afternoon. We drove out of the city's center, passing through Parco della Favorita, which Norman Lewis had described affectionately as prowling grounds for prostitutes, who, back then at least, were called *lucciole* (fireflies). All we saw was litter.

Eventually, we entered a bright spacious compound of failed cubist housing. Long straight streets stretched with small-windowed apartments. There were openings to the fresh air, but they didn't extend outward (like balconies), they burrowed inward (like snipers' nests). The monotony was broken in places by elevated sections rising sometimes as high as seven stories. You could see the hand of an architect; in fact, ZEN 2 reminded me vaguely of Moshe Safdie's Habitat 67, the still-in-use residence from Canada's world's fair, but a Habitat that had been pulled taut instead of honeycombed, and then left to fester.

At lunch the day before, Maruzza had downplayed the danger, and she drove through the compound with seeming nonchalance. Residents passed us on the street—there were more people loitering than driving cars—but few paid us any attention. I looked at them, though. After all the talk about the Mafia I wanted to see a Mafioso. I felt a bit like V. S. Naipaul, traveling through the South on a mission to find a redneck.

The compound was brittle but it wasn't ghastly. It takes a lot to impress an American with your slum, and here the corner rappers were replaced by girls on bikes. Also, the place was drenched in sunshine. Giuseppe di Lampedusa wrote in *The Leopard* that not even "the vibrant Sicilian light" could disperse Palermo's pervasive sense of death. But here it helped diminish an atmosphere of menace.

We parked by the church and entered the annex. The priest had offered a work space to Maruzza and her women, who were currently on summer hiatus. Padre Miguel was not in, so we took a walk along the piazza. The word carries such stately connotations for a foreigner that it sounded odd when applied to a vacant, garbage-strewn lot whose only inhabitants were two mangy dogs.

Maruzza pointed to the building running along its edge. "Many of the women I work with live there," she said. She had started the project two years earlier, teaching the women to make luxury handbags. Although the bags had different designs, they each carried the label: LABZEN^2, like a declaration of faith, or a sign of radical chic.

Most of the bag makers were married to Mafiosi who didn't appreciate their wives working, going out of the house, acquiring a feeling of empowerment. "They don't like me," Maruzza said with blithe resignation.

Within ZEN 2 were production centers for drugs. Kids were recruited as couriers and residents of Palermo made the trip out to do their shopping. It was the old sad story of hopelessness and crime, here combated by a pragmatist with a penchant for bags.

On the drive back to Palermo, Maruzza said she'd get me a meeting with the owner of Antica Focacceria San Francesco. Then we made a stop for gelato.

~

Thursday morning, Edoardo came by the SoleLuna to continue our talk that had been interrupted by the tour group. (I was meeting them later for lunch.)

We sat in the living room, the French doors of the balcony open to the heat. I told Edoardo that I'd been to ZEN 2. He said that the Mafia doesn't like that the schools are there, and added that the teachers have to fight against the culture of the parents. When I mentioned the piazza, he remarked: "It doesn't look like Italy. It looks like a Middle East place." He mentioned a plan—a dream?—to build a garden park there. "If you want to be effective in the fight against the Mafia, you have to create something that can be used in the poorest neighborhoods. If you give them the idea that they have a garden there because of the anti-Mafia, that can be helpful."

Edoardo told me that, while Addiopizzo began its life by recruiting members, it now waits for business owners to come to it. One man, a publican in the town of Caccamo, wrote to Addiopizzo quite distraught. He had gone to the police with the name of his extortionist, and in the process lost most of his customers. Edoardo, along with some colleagues, drove out to his pub to have a beer—a gesture he called "an act of ethical consumerism." And they continued going, every Saturday night, taking friends with them so they filled the place.

They started organizing parties there. This made an impression on the youth of Caccamo. Normally for nightlife, people from Caccamo go to Palermo.

Edoardo noted that in the old days paying protection money was a given. "There was no proof that it was possible not to pay. The young people starting businesses today—or taking over the business of their parents—they have a completely different idea. Fifteen years ago, if you thought about not paying protection money you thought about Libero Grassi. Now you think about the 460 who don't pay."

I asked Edoardo what he thought of the Mafia souvenirs— black T-shirts with pictures of Marlon Brando, caps with "Kiss My Hand" in Italian—that one sees in Palermo's tourist shops. "They are twisting the image of the Mafia," he said. "They are focusing on picturesque aspects. If Americans come with this idea they have no idea what the Mafia is. Making money with these *Godfather* shirts is to me a crime.

"In Corleone," he said, referring to the town some forty miles south of Palermo, "they sell Don Corleone liqueur. They organize Mafia tours. It's very fake. The most serious thing is they don't say a word about what the Mafia was—and still is. And they don't talk about the anti-Mafia movement." He said that Addiopizzo also takes tourists to Corleone, but instead of the bar, they show them the anti-Mafia museum, which was opened by the mayor in 2000.

"He understood that the only way to overcome the bad past in Corleone was to do an activity against the Mafia. Of course, he had bodyguards." I asked Edoardo if his parents worried about him.

"Yes," he said. "They are proud, but at the same time worried. They say, 'You should be prudent.'

"I would be worried if Addiopizzo lost the support of the people. That's a situation when the Mafia could attack because we'd be isolated. Libero Grassi was completely isolated. The Sicilian Industrialists' Association criticized him, saying he should not make so much noise. Now the Industrialists' Association supports Addiopizzo, and expels members who pay the pizzo.

"We really think that right now it's unlikely that the Mafia will attack us. Addiopizzo is under the spotlight. The backfire would hurt them. But," he added, "the strategy can change very quickly."

~

Edoardo headed off to another appointment and I made my way to Via Vittorio Emanuele, where I was meeting the group, for one last time, at the store that sold only pizzo-free products. It was easy to find; a large yellow and green sign over the door read: Punto Pizzo Free with the words L'Emporio underneath it. Unlike the small decal on the door of the Renato Bar, this signage stuck out like a boast (or even a taunt). I wondered how many English-speaking tourists walked in looking for a free slice of pizza.

Inside, a petite young woman with a bright round face sat behind the cash register. She had an openness that I'd seldom seen in Palermo shop assistants, and I pictured the most hardened Mafioso wandering in and immediately melting. It would be like trying to extort money from your kid sister.

Valeria said that it was her husband, Fabio, who had gotten the idea for a store that specialized in products from pizzo-free enterprises. Business was good, she said; when the store opened, a couple years earlier, it had received wide-spread coverage that had brought in locals, as well as tourists from abroad. "When people ask if we are afraid, we say we are so exposed all over the world, so we feel protected." The shield of notoriety, like the shield of popularity.

In addition to the shop, Valeria and her husband had started an agency that organized pizzo-free events. "We had a pizzo-free wedding," she exclaimed. "Flowers, photographer, singer, hotel." While sharing in her obvious joy at their accomplishment, I was nevertheless struck by how much of a Sicilian's life is—unless one works at it—connected to the Mafia.

On the wall hung a quote from Giovanni Falcone, which Valeria translated: "Man passes, but ideas remain.... Everyone has to continue to do his part, big or small; everyone has to make his contribution to improve the living conditions of Palermo."

The group arrived, with reddened shoulders and sun-kissed hair, looking finally like real tourists—the result of a morning swim in the sea. They roamed around the store, examining the cheeses and pastas, the teas and chocolates, the soaps and lotions, the jars of pesto and pine nuts, the bottles of wine and olive oil. There were shelves of *coppole*—which Edoardo had told us were the caps traditionally worn by Sicilians before the Mafia appropriated them as its symbol— and shelves of books. There were even two computers, providing pizzo-free Internet access.

Eventually, we made our way down a side street to Antica Focacceria San Francesco. As on Sunday, no armed guards stood in front. We took the stairs to the second floor and commandeered three tables under large black-and-white photographs. The place was packed, we were a group of twelve, and I hadn't yet met the owner. Yet out of the chaos emerged, in fairly short order, drinks for everyone followed by croquettes of mashed chickpeas followed by numerous pastas and a few of the famous cow spleen sandwiches. (Spleen, I discovered on trying my neighbor's, tastes pretty much as you'd expect spleen to taste.) We concluded our final meeting with a dozen larger-than-life cannoli.

~

In the evening, I took the bus out to Falcone-Borsellino Airport and picked up my suitcase, which had remarkably been brought back from oblivion. Returning to the city, I deposited it in my room and then headed out for a celebratory meal. A small crowd stood outside a pizzeria on Piazza Castelnuovo, including a trio speaking accented English. I asked them if the place was good, and the shorter of the two men told me it had the best pizza in Palermo. And that, he said, was coming from a Neapolitan. He introduced me to his friends, a young couple from Paris, and invited me to join them.

Still giddy over the reunion with my suitcase, I babbled about my week so far. The Parisians looked more impressed than the Neapolitan. After we were seated, I asked him what he was doing in Palermo.

"I am a *carabinieri* captain," he said.

He had wanted an assignment in Milan; he got Palermo instead. He knew ZEN 2. Although I'd been told the police didn't go near the place, he had been there fairly recently with a large unit.

"This is a terrible period for Italy," he said in a gruff, rapid-fire voice. "People are stupid—they watch TV and they believe what they hear. They don't read books. It takes too much time."

I brought up the Mafia. He said that, after the killings of Falcone and Borsellino, the Mafia realized it couldn't beat the state, so it decided to infiltrate it. "The sergeants are in Palermo," he said. "The generals are in Rome."

"You mean the politicians?" the Frenchman asked.

"Yes," he said coldly.

~

Padre Miguel made a rare trip into town to meet me for lunch, though he ordered only juice. With apologies, he explained that he'd been testifying in court the day of my visit. I expressed an interest but, he insisted, that was all he could say. Then he looked around the outdoor terrace of the Bar Aluia, just off the upscale Via della Libertà, and said with a smile: "This is not Palermo."

He appeared to be in his late thirties, a handsome man of easy-going warmth and uncommon fortitude. He wore a white short-sleeved shirt with a Roman collar. He was Argentinean, born of

153

Italian parents, and had studied Biblical languages in Rome. He had been teaching in the capital when, in 2008, he was assigned to San Filippo Neri parish in ZEN 2. "I am a priest," he said, "but also a missionary."

Of the six thousand families in ZEN 2, half, he said, did not have work—"legal, ordinary work," he clarified. "Children don't study. Boys stop going to school after the fifth grade.

"There are people forty and fifty years old who don't know the cathedral. Boys who don't know the sea. And it is two kilometers away.

"You can't talk of culture. You can't talk of foreign countries. The newspaper doesn't exist." His tone was not one of self-pity, but rather disheartenment at the barren lives of others.

The place, he said, was built like a castle, shut off from the rest of the world. "Inside the ZEN quarter you feel there is no Italy. Palermo doesn't invest in our neighborhood to get people to become citizens." Still, politicians periodically show an interest. "Some," he said, "pay fifty euros for a vote."

That payoff paled in comparison to the five hundred euros a kid could make selling cocaine for a night. Padre Miguel said that a carabinieri station was going to open soon, and that that would deter Palermitanos from coming out to buy drugs.

"There are many good people, good families," he insisted, estimating that of the thirty thousand people that live in the two ZENs, possibly a thousand were connected to the Mafia. He noted that they had one of the youngest populations in Italy. "We have six hundred children in catechism classes."

I asked him about the difficulty of his work.

"You can forget that you are a priest," he said. "You can think that you are a social worker. We must do social work, but as priests."

He said that he and his two fellow priests always dressed in clerical garb, and not as a personal reminder. "People respect priests," he said. "They like priests." He noted that people like Maruzza, as well as NGOs, do good work in the neighborhood, but they always leave at the end of the day. "We are the only ones that live there," he said. "And that's a big difference. But that's why people feel that we love them. Because we are like them."

That, however, didn't prevent a resident from trying to kill him. He dropped this piece of news casually and explained it dispassionately, saying that it was a man—not a Mafioso—who was trying to do something that would bring him attention. I assumed this was why he'd been testifying in court. I asked if he knew the people involved.

"Yes," he said. "I live with them. We are a family." He smiled, and then laughed. "A special family."

~

There was one more person I wanted to see in Palermo, and on one of my last days in the city, I made my way down now familiar streets to Antica Focacceria San Francesco. On the way, I stopped at L'Emporio to say hello to Valeria and to buy my sole Sicilian souvenir: a white T-shirt imprinted with a drawing of a tombstone inscribed *'U Pizzu* and backed by a crowd of cheering children.

Inside the restaurant, I asked at the register for Vincenzo Conticello. There must have been something about my pronunciation and my tortoiseshell glasses that marked me as harmless, because the man, after only a slight hesitation, pointed outside to two men sitting at a table under an umbrella just in front of the Focacceria café.

I waited for him to finish his meeting, sipping mineral water at a nearby table and coveting the life of a restaurateur. The slap on the back, the run of the kitchen. After twenty minutes he joined me, and I asked him about the history of the place. It was a beautiful summer afternoon, why darken it with more talk of the Mafia?

The Focacceria opened in 1834, he told me, and had been in his family for five generations. When he and his brother took over in the eighties, they expanded the menu—adding pastas and fish—and put tables in the piazza. "Before, this was used for parking," he said, "and rubbish. There was rubbish everywhere."

I mentioned—as a sign of further progress—that the last picture I had seen of the restaurant showed armed guards standing in front.

"They're still here," he said quickly, "now in plainclothes. Look behind you."

I turned and saw two fit young men sitting at a table and conversing quietly. I'd seen them earlier, and hadn't given them a thought. It was like putting on new glasses—seeing the world as it is.

"I have four bodyguards with me twenty-four hours a day," Vincenzo said, with a look of chagrin. "Three more work in the piazza. I don't come here very often," he added. "It's not safe."

It all started in 2005, when he found a letter in his car demanding that he pay fifty thousand euros and indicating that the price of refusal would be his life and that of his family. Then one day a Mafioso visited the Focacceria; he was later arrested (the police had had the restaurant under surveillance). Vincenzo attended the man's trial and identified him as his extortionist.

"Palermo is a very complicated town to work in," Vincenzo said, demonstrating a great gift for understatement. His cat was killed and his business suffered. Remembering the crowd at lunch the other day, I expressed surprise.

"Many people in Palermo that like the Mafia don't come to Focacceria," he explained. "Especially politicians. And owners of shops that pay the pizzo." He said that a lot of his business comes from foreign tourists and students, who attend the university or the international school.

Vincenzo had had big plans for expansion—in Italy and elsewhere—but the events of 2005 had sapped his energy, which he said was only starting to return.

I asked Vincenzo if he had any children. "A daughter," he said. She was no longer living in Sicily, and he didn't identify her new home. "To see my daughter is very complicated," he said wearily. "I must make four or five reservations in different towns."

The price one pays for living with dignity.

The waiter approached and Vincenzo translated the day's pasta specials. I ordered the spaghetti with tomatoes, swordfish, and mint. When he was gone, I asked Vincenzo about vacation.

"I prefer to take my vacation outside Italy," he said. "Because in Italy it would be with carabinieri."

He estimated that 20 to 25 percent of Sicilians are connected to the Mafia, but that another 25 percent have "a Mafioso mentality." He said it would take generations for the situation to improve. "Mentality is very difficult to change. The teachers in the schools work well," he said, echoing Edoardo. "But the families don't do the same at home."

We sat quietly for a while, then Vincenzo leaned forward and said sotto voce: "This man is a killer."

The words registered, but barely. I looked up as a hulking man in a white T-shirt and red suspenders lumbered past our table. Before he had even reached the street, Vincenzo motioned to the guard who had been standing watchfully by the café entrance. They exchanged words, the only one of which I understood was a sharp *"Attenzione."* Then Vincenzo got on his cell phone to another guard, one of the two who had been sitting behind me and who now stood in front of the Focacceria, into which the brute had just walked.

I had seen my Mafioso—unfortunately, while dining with a man the mob despised.

Vincenzo continued talking on his cell phone, amassing his men. He was visibly riled, which made me even more nervous. In a matter of seconds, the Mafia had moved from being a distant notion, an endless topic of discussion, to a graspable reality (the man had passed within inches of our table), a galvanic presence in red suspenders. Suddenly the idea of gunfire strafing a café—a familiar trope of gangster movies—seemed not at all far-fetched.

Our pastas arrived, adding, I couldn't help but think, another potential cinematic cliché.

The commotion put a damper on our conversation. Each of us sat with his own private thoughts, though our fates, for the moment at least, were inextricably tied.

"He killed four people," Vincenzo said finally, adding that he'd recently been released from prison after fifteen years. "He is a terrible Mafioso."

I mentioned that I'd seen him enter the Focacceria.

"Yes," Vincenzo said, a bit more calmly. "He looks here. He looks in there. He studies."

After finishing his pasta, Vincenzo explained that he had another appointment. He apologized, and insisted that I stay for dessert. I thanked him for his time, and then watched him climb into the backseat of a squad car, followed by his bodyguards. I hoped some of their colleagues were sticking around.

The waiter appeared shortly, bearing the dessert tray like a frothy distraction. I chose the *gelo di melone*, another specialty of Sicily. It was delicious, but I ate it warily.

Heaven of the Bavarians

A German beer festival—THE German beer festival—was the last place I expected to find emotional connection.

Germans, as I've written, I tended to meet on the road. When I was a newspaper travel editor, looking at a map of Europe and trying to decide where to go next, my eyes would usually pass over Germany. Italy? Any time. Sweden? In summer, gladly. Poland? Poland had become like a second homeland. Germany, even though I'm part German, never held great appeal for me. I had heard all about German rigidity, seriousness, the love of order—qualities that generally work to the advantage of the inhabitants (hence the country's popularity with immigrants) but not necessarily tourists. Sometimes, the countries that are the most comfortable to live in are the least interesting to visit. (Because it's the comfortably well-off who travel, and they want, naturally, to see something different.)

Beer, I thought, might make a difference, so in 2006 I went to Okto-berfest. It did make a difference, but I also needed serendipity. At least as much luck as beer was involved.

Remember this.

The vast hall. The great din. The spilled beer. The smoky haze. The saccharine music. The pretzel vendors. The workhorse waitresses. The buttery smell of roasted chickens. The vendors of silly hats. The bodies squeezed onto benches that disappear into the distance and suggest a school cafeteria of colossal scope and questionable fare. The strange feeling—as you drink engulfed by a human sea—of escape, of having departed the world of work, responsibility, sobriety. (Greatly heightened if it's a weekday.) The sense of ceremony and import given, through songs and toasts and the monumental scale, to a frat boy's passion. The private party of your table, in a humming hangar of tables, in a makeshift city of hangars, that survives new arrivals and silent departures and flows almost seamlessly from day into night. Your total ignorance of day or night. The young woman opposite you who presses her glass mug to her dirndled bosom and says with an ingenuous, combustible smile: "I love Oktoberfest!"

This, I'll remember.

~

"The thing about dirndls," Emile said, "is that they make average women look pretty and pretty women look beautiful."

It was Saturday morning in Munich, the opening day of Oktoberfest, and we were riding the U4 train to Theresienwiese. At each station more people boarded. Some of the men sported lederhosen, while many of the women wore aproned dresses atop low-cut blouses. The women's aprons and skirts coordinated in color (red and green, pink and brown) and the short-sleeved blouses were a frilly white. Lengths varied, for both pants and skirts, though younger men seemed to prefer longer lederhosen, while younger women often favored shorter hemlines.

"If the apron is tied on the left side," Emile explained, "it means you're married. If it's tied in the middle, you have a boyfriend, but if something better comes along . . ."

"And if it's tied on the right?" I asked.

He grinned. "It means you're open to anything."

It seemed odd to be getting a lesson in ethnography on a subway in Germany's most technologically advanced region. Earlier, Emile had told me the saying, "Bavaria is between lederhosen and laptops."

"I went to the hairdresser this morning," Emile said, "and the man who cut my hair was wearing lederhosen. People put on the clothes even if they're not going to Oktoberfest. It's a way for them to wear traditional stuff without anyone laughing at them."

Another station, another dash of dirndls.

Emile wore the classic jacket, or *janker*, over jeans. He was a Dutchman, the manager of a local hotel, and he obviously didn't feel the need to go all out. The gray jacket had a green collar and a pleat in the back; it was 95 percent wool and 5 percent cashmere. The buttons, he said, were traditionally made from deer antlers. His blue-and-white checked shirt echoed the Bavarian flag.

At Theresienwiese, the doors slid open and the world's most picturesque straphangers poured out. A stationmaster's announcement accompanied the flow: "Don't push, people. There's more than enough time to drink beer."

The escalator lifted us into sunlit fairgrounds: the fanciful shapes of funhouses, the childhood aroma of candied peanuts. It was, after the subway, like having ascended from hell into heaven. Emile led me down an avenue lined with rides and booths, some piled with pretzels, others hung with heart-shaped gingerbreads drizzled with icing inscriptions.

We entered the Ochsenbraterei "tent" (really a building), its tables already occupied by people drinking what looked like lager and stout.

Emile had told me that no beer is served until the mayor of Munich ceremoniously taps the first keg at noon. (People make bets on how many hits it will take him to do it.)

"They're drinking apple juice with mineral water," Emile explained. "And the dark stuff is Coke with Fanta."

Then he showed me the open kitchen, a huge ox turning on an industrial-strength spit. In a glass case, carved beef sandwiches already awaited whetted hungers while, to the side, rows of countless chickens roasted.

We exited the side and emerged onto a kind of midway, where ample cupids aimed arrows atop columns. Crowds three and four deep lined both sides as the Oktoberfest parade entered the grounds: bands, dignitaries, brewery wagons drawn by horses, their wooden kegs topped, occasionally, by platforms crammed with dirndled young women hoisting beer mugs with glee. It was interesting to see innocent joy, and a proud culture, built around a beverage that elsewhere gets associated with binges and louts. On the subway Emile had told me about the Strong Beer Festival, which is held in Munich every winter. In the old days, he had said, monks brewed beer rich in nutrition to drink during their fasts. Bavarians still say that "beer is not alcohol, it is liquid bread."

We headed off for our daily bread.

Cutout clouds hung from a blue-and-white striped ceiling, the celestial colors of Bavaria. Above the garlanded bandstand, which revolved in the middle of a peopled plain, hung the words HIMMEL DER BAYERN (Heaven of the Bavarians). A great hum; a soft roar; that seldom heard sound of mass conviviality unconnected to a game or anything outside itself reverberated off walls painted with scenes of old Munich.

We had entered the Hacker Festzelt (Hacker festival tent). The major Munich breweries have their own "tents" at Oktoberfest—during the parade, Emile had pointed out the pedestaled Löwenbräu lion—and each tent has a specific character. Hacker is known for its excellent band, Augustiner for its unparalleled beer. Hofbräu is popular with foreigners, so locals tend to avoid it. "It's just drinking," Emile said, by which

I assumed he meant "getting drunk." Pschorr-Bräurosl has a reputation as a party tent. "On Monday the mayor welcomes Munich's gay community there." Wine lovers are accommodated in the Weinzelt. Celebrities and VIPs gravitate to Käfer and Hippodrom. "Boris Becker comes to Oktoberfest," Emile said. "He wears lederhosen." It was easy to picture in lederhosen one of the last male tennis players who wore tight shorts.

Emile led me past waitresses—who were already racing around with roasted chickens—and into a raised alcove set with clothed tables. It was like a little restaurant off to the side, a corporate box removed from the clamor of the pit. We joined four of his colleagues at their table by the wall.

Thirsty cheers greeted the mayor's keg tap; soon beers in dimpled glass mugs arrived. We toasted before tasting, each person curling a liter of liquid and making sure to look the others in the eye.

"If you don't make eye contact when you toast," Emile said, "you'll have seven years of bad sex."

The taste was weighty and smooth. The beer at Oktoberfest, a German had told me, is stronger than regular beer but it tastes weaker.

"The beer is a little weaker than regular beer," Emile said, "but it tastes stronger."

The waitresses scurried, the band played, the table gabbed. The young man next to me had been born in Hungary, the man next to him was a German who had converted to Islam (he was sticking with the Coke and Fanta), and the dirndled woman opposite, with the warm smile, was a Slovak who had grown up in Uruguay. Conversation halted as the band began a new song; mugs clinked, eyes locked (briefly, but critically), everyone sang:

Ein Prosit, ein Prosit
Der Gemütlichkeit
Ein Prosit, ein Pro-o-sit
Der Gemüt-lich-keit.

"A toast, a toast to *gemütlichkeit*"—one of those priceless German words that defines a feeling often unacknowledged by other languages, in this case a kind of warm, happy, cozy friendliness.

A middle-aged couple arrived, Ines in dirndl, Dieter in sport coat and blue-and-white checked tie. They placed on the table heart-shaped chocolates tied to ribbons.

"They give them to the waitress," Emile said, before explaining the symbiotic relationship that develops between server and served at Oktoberfest. In a taproom that holds 6,900 people, it pays to get on good terms with your waitress.

Dieter took off his sport coat; Emile removed his *janker*; I rolled up my sleeves. Beads of sweat ran down my face.

"When the weather is good," Dieter said, "it's bad for Oktoberfest."

There was no air-conditioning and no ventilation. The windowless walls trapped kitchen aromas, cigarette smoke, body heat. The massive tents went up at the end of every summer for the sixteen-day flurry—this year eighteen due to German Reunification Day—and then were dismantled and stored for another year. But all was not as ephemeral as it appeared.

"If you're the host of a tent," Emile explained, "you immediately become a millionaire." However, to be anointed you had to be a restaurateur.

Our waitress, now wearing her red-wrapped chocolates around her neck, passed out menus. Almost everyone ordered chicken.

"Chicken," Emile said, "is what you traditionally eat at Oktoberfest."

It arrived shortly—a crispy brown bird with surprisingly salty, buttery skin and succulent meat. It made you want to drink more beer and never eat an American chicken again.

"They're happy chickens," Dieter said to me laughing.

The Slovak shared her plate of sausage and sliced radish. I ate a curl to the tune of "La Bamba."

"This band is great," Emile said. "They play everything from marches to disco. Later in the evening they'll do AC/DC."

"When I hear 'New York, New York,'" Dieter said, "I know I'm at Oktoberfest."

A vendor appeared with her collection of hats, including a huge one shaped like a keg.

"*Ein Prosit, ein Prosit* . . ."

Forks dropped, mugs rose, eyes met.

"They play that song about every fifteen minutes."

"So you keep drinking."

The host stopped by—a modest-looking millionaire in the making—and welcomed us to his tent.

"I'll come out here about twelve, thirteen times before it's over," Emile said, after the host had gone. Some of that was for work—entertaining clients, socializing with employees. Office staffs in Munich often pick a day to spend at Oktoberfest. What finer way to boost worker morale? Who needs management strategies when you have *gemütlichkeit*?

"*West Virginia, mountain mama* . . ."

"On the last evening," Emile said, "they turn the lights off and everyone holds sparklers. It's quite dramatic."

Emile's dirndled wife arrived with two friends and sat at the table behind ours.

"*Well it's one for the money, two for the show, three to get ready now go cat go* . . ."

A new round of beers appeared.

"*. . . but don't you, step on my blue suede shoes.*"

Followed by bowls of apple strudel swimming in vanilla sauce.

"*There she was just a-walkin' down the street* . . ."

Everyone seemed to know every word of every song, and I remembered that, after the war, Munich had been in the American Zone.

"*. . . singin' do wah diddy diddy dum diddy do.*"

I excused myself to go to the men's room.

"*Ein Prosit, ein Prosit . . .*"

About ten yards out, a mini-million-man march had begun. I eased myself into its flow, and let the current sweep me slowly toward the lavatory. We burst through the doorless entrance and spilled into a noisy estuary, guys splintering off down busy channels banked by trickling troughs. Songs in German broke out in accompaniment. And relief. I looked up at one point to find, shockingly close, the face of the similarly occupied young man opposite. Job done, I rejoined the current, briefly impeded by soapless sinks, and was carried outside.

Back at the table sweat dripped. Beer flowed. Music played. Hours passed. Time stopped. On the main floor, people were already starting to dance on the benches. Emile and company got up to leave. I said goodbye, then joined two couples at a neighboring table. I was working.

"*Ein Prosit, ein Prosit . . .*"

"You have to look everybody in the eye . . ." said Bettina, the woman in the green dirndl.

". . . or you'll have seven years of bad sex," I finished her sentence.

"I had that once," said one of the men, looking despondently into his beer.

We rolled over to the Bräurosl tent, the whole place a-swirl with dancing bodies. Squeezing onto a bench, we flailed, swayed, and stumbled with the crowd. My shirt got its first taste of the beverage I'd been drinking since noon.

Then, abruptly, the music stopped. The sudden diminution of noise was as brutal as its opposite. It was eleven o'clock; time had not stopped after all. The band started packing up their instruments, people resignedly began filing out. The long, sodden, happily wasted day was over.

Not so fast. My new friends led me outside (fresh air!) down a wobbly concourse (easy does it!) and up to a small stage where a collection of costumed characters stood. A barker in lederhosen jumped up and down to carnival music. The sign above him read: AUF GEHT'S BEIM SCHICHTL.

A magic show, Bettina explained, an Oktoberfest tradition. "It's so bad," she said as we took our seats inside, "that it's good."

And it was. I didn't understand a word, yet I laughed so loudly I nearly fell off the bench. Of course, this was after four liters of beer.

~

Three days later I put on my blue-and-white checked shirt and took the subway back to Theresienwiese. I didn't feel the pressure I had felt on Saturday. (Travel writer pressure is a little-discussed subject.) I'd already gotten enough material for a story, but I knew I had seen only a sampling. Today I wanted to wander, poke around on my own, add a macro to my micro view. It seemed right to fatten a story about an event known for excess. Didn't a festival that saw the consumption of six million liters of beer, 560,000 pork knuckles, 480,000 chickens, and 360,000 sausages deserve, at the least, an additional two thousand words?

A cool rain fell on inert amusements and dripping parkas ducked into tranquil tents. Tuesday morning at Oktoberfest. I remembered Dieter's comment, that good weather was bad for Oktoberfest, and hoped the opposite was also true.

Ochsenbraterei was doing the best business. "Our tent is for people who come for our famous ox," a waiter told me. "It's mainly an eating tent."

Pinky was from Austria. "We're all from Austria," he said, motioning to his colleagues relaxing at tables in a rare moment of calm. He had been coming for fifteen years, driving across the border and renting an apartment with friends. It was fun, he said, and you made good money if you got good tips. A lot of the wait staff did the same, working Oktoberfest before the start of the ski season back home. "They like our Austrian hospitality," Pinky said.

He looked like a young Bill Murray in lederhosen. "This was my grandfather's. It's similar to German lederhosen but the stitching is white—that's Tyrolean. Bavarian stitching is yellow or green." The International League of Leather Shorts.

On my way out, I talked to a blond restroom attendant. She was from St. Petersburg, Russia, and wore a white smock.

Walleyed pike grilled on sticks outside Fischer-Vroni, and toy horses hung from suspended wheels in the awakening Hippodrom. A cook from Mozambique took a break in the Augustiner-Festhalle, which was a break from his regular job at a Munich hospital. In a service shed outside Käfer, more mountain chalet than bannered beer hall, a sweat-shirted wait staff huddled from the rain. I asked the young woman what she was reading.

"*The Peter Principle*," she said. "I'm an economics student."

A dozen apostates sipped in the doldrums of the Weinzelt. A well-meaning German had warned me—like an American advising a foreign visitor not to talk soccer—"You don't drink wine at Oktoberfest." But I had wanted to see for myself.

The rain fell harder. I trotted back to the Augustiner tent, thinking that the great thing about Oktoberfest was its complete dismissal of the outside world. Still, I couldn't help but wonder if Saturday had been my day.

The middle section was filling quickly. I walked up and down a number of aisles, a number of times, searching for a table that looked interesting, friendly, quotable. I spotted one, with a good dirndl-and-lederhosen quotient, only to hear when I reached it American accents. (A store near my hotel was doing a brisk business selling kits to tourists, and I'd occasionally see young men strutting about the neighborhood in their newfound Teutonicness.) Close by, another group looked promising, but all its members were shrouded in smoke. Near the end of the aisle stretched an empty table. Recklessly, I took a seat.

I ordered bratwurst with sauerkraut and a beer, then scored a pretzel from a passing vendor. It was 1:30. I was the only person in the now populous hall eating alone. Oh, I thought, the Oktoberfest stories I will tell.

Lunch arrived—four links of sausage atop a bed of cabbage—followed by two young women in dirndls. They asked, I think, if the seats opposite me were free. I nodded profusely. I lost my appetite.

"Do you speak English?" I asked.

"Yes," they said.

Pia worked in a bar in Schwabing (the once artistic, now affluent neighborhood where I had stayed my first days in Munich); Teresa in a restaurant on the way to the airport. I asked if they ever thought about working Oktoberfest.

"No," said Teresa, shaking her brown curls. "The women who work Oktoberfest are tough. It's hard work—you work eighteen straight days. But if you get good tips, you can go half a year without working."

"If you don't tip enough for the first beer," Pia instructed me, "you have a long wait for the second."

Their beers arrived; we clinked glass mugs.

"You have to look the other person in the eye," Teresa said, "or you'll have seven years of bad sex."

There was something about hearing this instruction from an attractive young woman that made the adjective of the outcome fade in importance. And the noun grow.

"We usually go to the Schottenhamel Festhalle," Teresa said. "That's where the young people go. But the beer at Augustiner is the best."

She put a cigarette to her lips and held it there, unlit, for a few seconds, looking a bit like Jeanne Moreau in *Jules et Jim*. She was starting studies in psychology after Oktoberfest, while Pia was traveling to Australia with a friend. Pia had been a national wrestling champion in high school, but she didn't wrestle anymore. I asked what she did for exercise.

"Nothing," she said.

Teresa looked around (I feared for a new table), sitting erect and taking it all in: the darting waitresses, the buoyant melodies, the tightly-bunched benches (apart from ours), the soaring tangle of a thousand conversations, the mega-*gemütlichkeit*. Then she gripped her beer mug, pressed it to her bosom, and said, beaming: "I love Oktoberfest!"

A few minutes later, a young woman in a dirndl sat next to me. This was Sabine, who was going to Australia with Pia. She had met an Australian during the World Cup. Everyone around the table agreed that Germany's hosting of the tournament that summer had been a wonderful moment, not just for romance. They confirmed what I'd read in the papers, that Germans had enjoyed, for the first time in decades, public displays of patriotism.

"Germany has this big weight on its shoulders," Teresa said sadly.

The frilly left sleeve of Sabine's blouse rose above a large purple patch.

"You come to Oktoberfest," Teresa said, "and the next morning you wake up and find bruises. Often you don't remember how you got them."

"*Ein Prosit, ein Prosit . . .*"

We all clinked mugs.

Another friend arrived and sat next to Pia. This was Charlotte, a law student. She was dressed in a blouse and jeans.

"I was studying for an exam this morning," she explained, "and I didn't want to wear a dirndl to the library." Then she added: "It feels strange to come here in regular clothes. You look like a tourist."

"There are exams during Oktoberfest?" I asked.

"After."

A fellow law student arrived, Olga from Poland, who took a seat to my left. My table was filling up nicely.

"Oktoberfest can have trouble," Teresa said. "There are always a few rapes."

"You don't walk down dark streets," Pia said.

"And if one of us gets drunk," said Teresa, "we stay together."

Somehow the hall, all its drama and color, had receded into the background until nothing existed beyond our table. Out of the surrounding tumult, we had carved an intimate space. I was aware of a general racket off in the distance, and of course the insistent intrusion, like a welcome alarm, that regularly brought us out of our world and back into the fold:

"*Ein Prosit, ein Prosit . . .*"

Putting down my mug, I asked if it was true that locals don't come to Oktoberfest on weekends.

"We came on Saturday," Teresa said. "It's a tradition to see the mayor tap the keg. But usually we don't come on weekends. Especially next weekend."

"Why?"

"It's Italian Weekend."

She told me that Italian men had a reputation at Oktoberfest for not being able to hold their alcohol, and for groping women. Those in dirndls, she said, were particularly vulnerable.

More beers arrived. Pia stuck her finger in Teresa's.

"What's this called in English?" she asked.

"The head."

"The Bavarians say if you drink it your breasts get bigger."

She licked her finger.

"There are always a lot of colds at Oktoberfest," said Teresa.

"People drinking from the same glasses," said Pia.

"And exhaustion," said Charlotte.

"Do you know how Oktoberfest started?" Teresa asked me.

"It was a celebration for the wedding of Prince Ludwig," I said.

"Very good. Most foreigners don't know that. They just think it's a big party."

"Is it true that Oktoberfest isn't as crowded as it used to be?" I asked.

"Yeah. Some people are worried about terrorism." I had noticed the absence of security checks.

Two men, inevitably, took seats at the empty end of our table. They were from London's East End. I could barely understand them.

"*Ein Prosit, ein Prosit . . .*"

"They want to know what *gemütlichkeit* means in English," Teresa told me.

"It's a kind of warm, happy, cozy friendliness," I told them.

"It's Bavarian," Teresa said smiling.

"No," Sabine corrected. "But it's typical of Bavaria."

I thought of other German words we use in English: kindergarten, gesundheit, wanderlust, schadenfreude.

"Schadenfreude," Teresa nodded. "That's a good one."

She wanted to know what I'd seen in Munich. I went down the list: Marienplatz, Viktualienmarkt, Englischer Garten, Dachau.

"By the time you're in high school," someone said, "you've been to Dachau four times."

"It's part of our history," Teresa said, not in a dismissive but an accepting way. Her tone suggested that its enormity was something that had been inculcated in her, something that she and all Germans had been made to come to terms with. At the same time, it was clear that she saw it as an aberration of the past.

Pia offered me her beer while I waited for mine. "I don't like beer," she said.

"You don't drink the last part," Teresa informed me as I got near the bottom. "It's not good. We call it *norgerl*. Last year Pia made a glass of it and sold it to an Italian."

Pia fiddled with her bodice.

"It's tight," she complained. "I bought it two years ago."

"And the more you drink," Sabine said, grinning, "the tighter it gets."

"Ein Prosit, ein Prosit . . ."

Quietly, people disappeared; a few—like the Brits—never to return. Teresa arrived back after a long absence with a rose nestled between her breasts. She talked of moving to another tent; I asked if it wasn't difficult finding seats. "We're girls," she said smiling, as if I'd forgotten.

A band of young men swooped in like musketeers. One had a dramatic wave of golden hair that went beautifully with his lederhosen.

"He's my ex-boyfriend," Teresa whispered.

"I hear you're a very interesting person," Tim said, squeezing in next to me.

"Three beers ago, perhaps." This is what I would have said if I'd had the clarity to think of it then.

"I want to buy you a beer."

We climbed up on the benches and started to dance. The music was still Bavarian. I kept scraping with my right heel the back of the woman seated behind me. She'd turn around and gaze up at me with half-hearted annoyance.

To her relief, the music stopped. I looked at my watch: 10:30, the weekday closing time. Then I looked around the table—the skyline of mugs, the crush of dirndls and lederhosen, the rose-scented breasts— and marveled at how it had changed in the course of nine hours.

Outside, the night was clear. Tim and his friends braved carnival rides.

"They're very drunk," said Charlotte.

"They don't look it," I said, though I was not the best judge.

"But they are. The last thing a boy wants to do is show he is drunk before a girl. But then we end up taking them back to their homes."

I made it on my own.

Later, I thought how Oktoberfest is a little like life. You enter it alone and you depart it alone (at least I did). At the beginning, you are fresh and alert, wide-eyed to the novelty and the grandness of it all. You eat and drink, you sing songs, you make friends; there are high points and lulls, triumphs and defeats. There are, for some people, periods of sickness. As time passes, your reactions slow, you slur your words, you walk a bit unsteadily. You get a sense it's all coming to a close. The music stops. You say your farewells.

Early Thursday morning, I rolled my suitcase through Viktualienmarkt, where a few vendors were already displaying their apples, and into the rare quiet of Marienplatz. I stood for a moment and took in the scene: the square washed in dawn's light, the New Town Hall noble and solitary minus the tourists. I thought: I'll probably never see this again. Then I stepped onto the escalator and descended to the subway. It was a common travel writer moment, conclusively turning my back on beauty. But there was solace in knowing that Munich would always glow for me, and Teresa would never age, remaining forever in my memory a carefree young woman clasping a beer to her breast and proclaiming her unquenchable passion for life.

Travels with a Book

One of the explanations some Americans give for not having passports is that there's so much to see here in the United States. And it's true. Ours is an extraordinarily rich country—culturally, ethnically, topographically. Easterners can drive to Utah or Arizona and see landscapes more alien than any they would find in Europe. However, if they've never been abroad, they can't fully grasp the uniqueness of the splendors they so admire.

As a travel writer who travels the world, I love traveling in the United States. There's the language: I not only understand the words, I also get the references, the nuances, the jokes. And there's the openness of Americans, something one especially appreciates after traveling in northern Europe, or in countries with a long history of repression.

American friendliness is nowhere more evident, perhaps, than in the Midwest. My first visit was in the eighties, to Chicago, where smiles and helpfulness seemed woven into the urban fabric. In 1992 I went on a road trip around Iowa, discovering kindness in every town. Both places appeared in my second book, and I did readings in both when I went out to promote it. By that time, 2005, I had visited dozens of countries, and was able to see the Midwest as the true, decent heart of my own.

Travel writers, regularly dismissed as trivialists, rarely indulge in the popular book tour whine. It's not just that we have bigger trips to fry, we have fewer bones to pick. We don't see what novelists find so objectionable about a diet of fine hotels, especially when the rooms all come reserved and generously paid for. We are puzzled by the memoirists' complaint about living out of a suitcase because to us it's infinitely preferable to living in the past. And, needless to say, we don't quite grasp the horror of going out and meeting readers. Those sensitive souls who flaunt their lack of social skills are as pathetic as people who boast that they are bad at math. A signing in Dubuque is not a journey into the heart of darkness.

The only possible trauma of a book tour is the potential encounter with apathy. The empty chairs of a ghostly chain at the short end of a mall in a town without pity. But for this, too, travel writers are much better prepared. We tend not to enter MFA programs, teach at universities, or live in New York City, so we are in constant touch with the great unread. From our hours spent in airports we know that most Americans, when presented with large chunks of free time and removed from demanding home entertainment systems, will find almost any excuse—a smartphone, a laptop, another bag of chips— not to pick up a book. Traveling, we're continually reminded of the growing homelessness of the written word.

So, unburdened by illusions and still out of the house, travel writers are the happiest authors on tour. Some may give the impression, often by their wardrobes, that they'd be much more content sharing gourds of gazelle blood with Maasai tribesmen, but don't believe them. A book tour provides us with a focus—not always a given in our all-over-the-map trade. And the focus, in another pleasing twist, is us.

Travel writers are, by nature, in search of the Other—which, by definition, is not oneself. It is only on a book tour that we stand front and center.

True, that position is difficult to define—not to mention enjoy— in an empty store. But all day long the evening reading gives us a sense of purpose, a handy response to Chatwin's ever-present "what am I doing here?" If it turns out to be a wash, there's always the sympathetic staff to chat with, and pump for local color. A stood-up author still beats a doubting travel writer, especially when they're one and the same.

I know because I've played the part. When my second book, *A Way to See the World*, came out in paperback, I traveled to the Midwest to revisit some of the places that appear in it. It was a self-guided tour—my publisher was small; I was even smaller—that, to the best-seller pashas, probably sounds as uplifting as a solo honeymoon. But they're not travel writers flying coach with their first paperback.

~

The shuttle from Midway buzzed with raves for warring weekend attractions. The young woman behind me announced that she had come to see the Red Sox play in a rare Wrigley Field appearance, while the two other women talked excitedly about the Blues Festival. It was good preparation for the Printers Row Book Fair which I wouldn't have received in a chauffeured limo.

The thing about great cities is that they have enough people to go around. On Saturday afternoon, crowds of nonfrequent flyers grazed the book tents on Dearborn Street. "Everybody's carrying about fifteen extra pounds right now," Carlos Cumpián, a local Chicano writer, explained to me as we sipped iced tea at a sidewalk café. "During the winter they're able to hide it under coats. Chicagoans look their best in October—after the summer, and before they've had their Halloween candy."

The evening VIP party was held in a parking lot. The unassuming locale carried a certain appeal which apparently only I appreciated, as almost no other authors attended. This was a disappointment. At the Miami Book Fair there had been a cocktail party in a downtown office tower that most of the featured authors attended. In Austin, the Texas Book Festival featured breakfast at the governor's mansion and a dinner with a dance band. The Arkansas Literary Festival in Little Rock hosted a black-tie gala that included a postprandial game of "Name That Tome" (my team lost to Roy Blount Jr.'s). Each had seemed a kind of glittery reward for the cloistered life that every author could treat as a personal celebration.

In Chicago, for whatever reason, authors felt no need to congregate. At least not in parking lots. I searched in vain for the black-and-white Hawaiian shirt of Paul Theroux, whom I had listened to in an airless tent a few hours earlier. He had flattered his audience, comprising about two hundred people (in a city of three million), congratulating them for being readers. They were, he said, "like the early Christians, gathering in tents." He told of talking to a young woman recently, a college graduate, and mentioning a book by Robert Louis Stevenson. She had never heard of him.

"Didn't your parents read to you when you were a child?" Theroux had asked her incredulously.

It occurred to me that writers' concerns about the decline of reading stem from more than just a self-preservation instinct; they are tied, as well, to the nearly-as-powerful need to connect. You don't have to read me, but read so you can talk to me. All writers were readers first, and most of us continue our lives as more prolific readers than writers; with fellow readers—unlike with fellow writers— we feel a noncompetitive bond. (There are no prestigious workshops, covetous magazine assignments, or Pulitzer Prizes for readers.) Tell a writer you write and depression sets in; tell a writer you read and gratitude blossoms.

I carried my plate of hummus and bruschetta and sat down at a table of secondhand booksellers. Used books were more a part of the Printers Row Book Fair than of the other fairs I'd been to. One of the sellers said there used to be even more secondhand stalls, before the chain bookstores became involved and inevitably changed the character of the fair. A woman with short brown hair and dirty fingernails told me, too, that many older, even middle-aged secondhand booksellers (middle-aged and secondhand—a dire combination in the country of the next new thing) gave up on book fairs because of the physical labor involved. Ultimately, there is a lot of heavy lifting in literature.

~

On Sunday, I woke up well before my 2:30 presentation. I was scheduled to appear with a professor of Buddhism who had written a book about the religion and his experiences teaching it in Cambodia. I was ambivalent about panels, not just because the audience is doubled for your potentially one-bettered performance, but because they had produced, at previous fairs, my greatest public debacle as a writer, and my finest hour.

In Miami, I had followed the author of a book about her multicultural neighborhood in Queens. She had brought slides, recordings, and her sizable talents as an actress and mimic, re-creating accents that ranged from rapper to Ukrainian immigrant. It was an impressive performance, and a long one, as the coauthor, her husband, hadn't been able to make the trip and she took the time allotted to (at least) two speakers. When she finally finished, and the lights came back on, a crew appeared to dismantle her audio and visual aids. During the lull, a large portion of the audience, either having seen what they'd come for or believing the session now over, got up and walked out, heartlessly passing in front of me as they went. The moderator, inexplicably at a loss, made no announcement. I watched the agonizing faces of friends who stayed and thereby magnified my humiliation by being witnesses to it. Eventually I took the podium and read a short section in a voice of controlled hurt.

In Austin, things worked out differently. As viewers of C-SPAN2's Book TV know, readings at the Texas Book Festival take place in the state capitol. My panel, probably because it contained two Texans, was put in the House Chamber. The three of us looked out from our hillock over a plush plain of leather swivel chairs, all of them occupied by make-believe legislators. Lesser would-be officials speckled the balcony.

Once again I went last, after another dramatic reading, this one by a young Hispanic woman who used not only her voice but her body to evoke a night of rumba in Havana. After she sat down, and the other Texan read—about the founder of a sailing ship company—I pulled out a newspaper column I'd written inspired by recent campaign speeches. (The book fair took place one week before the presidential election.)

"My fellow Americans," I said, "as your next president, I will ensure that every working man and woman receives one month of vacation a year."

Applause rang through the chamber.

"I will approve discounts on Prozac for flight attendants.

"I will make any hotel with attitude host a weekly Rotary Club luncheon.

"I will convince the manufacturers of suitcases to come up with a new black.

"I will pass through Congress a bill mandating that any passengers who fail to fit their carry-on bags into the overhead compartment on the first try must turn said bags over to a flight attendant and, before landing, write letters of apology to all the people with seats in the rows behind them."

The vote in the House was clear: I had carried Texas.

~

In Chicago, I met the professor of Buddhism in the authors' lounge. I had imagined a man who brought a bemused detachment to the huzzah of the marketplace, so I was relieved when he seemed as concerned about sales and publicity as I was. We were taken to a small classroom in which about twenty people sat. I read first, from my chapter on Comiskey Park, and then the professor read about Cambodia—two subjects that quite possibly had never been paired, and probably never should be again.

Afterwards, I signed three books and then looked on as the line, made up mostly of comely young women, grew in front of the professor's table. The majority of readers are female, of course, just as the majority of sports fans are male. (The percentage of women at a ball game is no doubt comparable to the percentage of men at a book fair.) The fact that I was in Chicago was no excuse for my choice of reading; people don't want to be transported to the homegrown. And as a meaningful way of life, Buddhism will always surpass support for the White Sox.

For ten long minutes I not only encountered apathy, I watched its opposite turn its perfumed back to me. Panels. Then I remembered that I was a travel writer and I did what travel writers do: I left. I walked out of the book fair, picked up my rental car, and pointed it toward Iowa.

~

I was looking forward to my first trip to the state since 1992. That also was an election year, and as in every election year, commentators were talking about the heartland. I had never been to the heartland. I flew to Des Moines, rented a car, and discovered a miscellany of intimate

Americana: the Surf Ballroom in Clear Lake where Buddy Holly, Ritchie Valens, and the Big Bopper gave their last performance; the National Hobo Convention in nearby Britt; the "Field of Dreams" in Dyersville; the limestone buildings of Grant Wood's old artists' colony in Stone City—everything connected by rolling fields of tall green corn. I thought of all the people who had said "Huh?" when I had told them where I was going next.

The sun disappeared as Copland's "The Red Pony" played on the radio. Just across the Mississippi a Super 8 motel sign pierced the gloaming. I dropped my bags in my room and headed into Le Claire. A 1923 Rolls-Royce sat in front of Sneaky Pete's.

"That's my car," said one of the two men sitting at the bar. "A Silver Ghost." He and his friend had left New Hampshire and were on their way to Montana for a little fly-fishing. In two years, he said, they were going to ship the car to China and then drive it in the Peking to Paris Motor Challenge.

Hundreds of neckties hung from the ceiling of the dining room. "We cut them off customers," the bartender told me, before mentioning that "Buffalo Bill" Cody had been born in Le Claire (somehow I had missed the town on that first trip). Minutes later he brought me my buffalo burger, which I washed down with a glass jar of beer.

"Where you staying?" he asked. "Out at the Super 8? That's too bad—I've got a B&B," and he handed me a card for the Hog Heaven Bed & Breakfast. I sat there struck (once again) by the limitless riches of the road—in fifteen minutes I had found four travel stories, that of a biker B&B being almost as marvelous as that of the future Eurasian road racers—and also by the brute similarities between the lodging and publishing industries. The franchises—Super 8, Paulo Coelho—get prominent placement along the highway and just inside the door (and with it ever increasing business), while the little guys—the B&Bs and midlist authors (while often charming and full of personality)—fight a losing battle tucked away on the side streets and back shelves where they are invisible to all except those who specifically seek them out. That night I cut my ties with the chain motels.

In Iowa City I found a handsome B&B in the middle of a leafy residential street. It was a good walk from the university, but I could still imagine professors heading off in the morning to disseminate knowledge. A visiting professor of mathematics, in fact, occupied the room next to mine. In the morning, we were joined at table by an innkeeping couple from Minneapolis, and in that easy familiarity of boarding house breakfasts, they asked about me. B&Bs, it was clear, give go-it-alone book tour authors not only a warm feeling of solidarity, but also an excellent opportunity for self-promotion. Front and center once again. And many people, moved either by a brush with celebrity or a bout of sympathy, will buy a book if they've met the author. At least they say they will.

~

A sign in the upstairs café at Prairie Lights (independent booksellers get the same professional courtesy as B&Bs) informs customers that they are on the site of the old literary society, The Times Club, that brought Robert Frost, Carl Sandburg, e.e. cummings, Langston Hughes, and Sherwood Anderson to town. Black-and-white photographs of them and others decorate the walls.

My reading was hosted by a local radio personality and carried live on WSUI. (As are all readings at Prairie Lights, giving them an unexpected air of import.) About fifty people filled the chairs, while a blessed handful stood in the back. Thanks be to college towns with famous writers' workshops. Ignoring the lessons of Chicago, I read about Iowa, though I ended with a soliloquy on the beauty of unsung places. When the hour-long program was over, a number of people came up to chat. (It was me or nothing.) One was a boy, no older than fourteen, who gave me my book to be signed and then, just as endearingly, his hand to be shaken.

~

The next morning I stopped in Anamosa to visit Grant Wood's grave, leaving a postcard of my book with the woman in the Chamber of Commerce office. (After verifying that I had correctly identified it as his final resting place.)

That night's reading in Dubuque was turned into a signing as the space before the microphone remained dishearteningly vacant. Friendly staff made like a grounds crew and swiftly moved my table out of the café and into the center aisle.

An author at a signing is like a picture at an exhibition—passively open to public scrutiny, ridicule, approval, dismissal, avoidance. The difference being, of course, that the author perceives and registers (or, frequently, tries not to register) the reactions she inspires. Sometimes he's simply an information source for the customer looking for the latest Palahniuk.

Our culture has no accepted etiquette for dealing with writers sitting alone with their books. People bring to the experience, even in large cities, no helpful guidelines or learned behaviors. Which is why I remember with such awe and affection the young woman in Dubuque.

She walked by, trailing her husband and two small children.

"So, you're an author," she said, slowing her pace but not coming to a stop.

"Yes," I said.

"Congratulations."

Acknowledgments

I wish to thank James Marcus, who read my essay on the joys of travel and thought it had the makings of a book. Thanks also to Rosecrans Baldwin, Roger Hodge, Evelyn Somers Rogers, and Philip Terzian, who all found in their publications a home for my writing.

I am grateful to Tony Lyons for his interest in the book—and his commitment to travel writing over the years—and to Jesse McHugh for his excellent editing.

The travel writing community is a remarkably supportive one, and I have benefitted greatly from my friendships with a number of its members, especially Pamela Petro, Ericka Hamburg, Alan Behr, Diane Mapes, Terry Ward, MB Roberts, Sally Shivnan, Don George, Jim Benning, Michael Yessis, Larry Habegger, David Farley, Rolf Potts, Eva Holland, Evan Balkan, Anne Kalosh, Doug Mack, Judith Gille, Dave Seminara, Ben Batchelder, Eric Weiner, and Pico Iyer.

I am indebted to friends near and far who have taken an interest in my writing (without ever prying): Jane Cowles & Dan Laskin, Sally Lane & Sam Graff, Jeanne & Peter Meinke, Monika & Jerzy Thieme, Ildikó & György Szőnyi, Lyn & Jesse Millner, Joanne & Don Dickerson, Betsy & Bob Pickup, Ela & Marek Kowalski, Claudine & Charles Campi, Christine & John Dolen, Cecile &

Mark Gauert, Ana & Ben Crandell, Debra & Greg Carannante, Donnette & Graham Donley, Katia Breslawec & Guy Peterson, Sonia Ortega Sanz, Agnieszka Baumritter, Elizabeth Sachs, Bibi Dumon Tak, Zofia Souche, Lilian Liang, Joe Recchi, Laura Recchi, Kate Pickup, Susan Puckett, Ellen Forman, Matt Schudel, Heather McKinnon, Daysi Calavia-Robertson, Mitchell Kaplan, Cristina Nosti, Gretchen Fletcher, Yinjie Qian, Monika Regulska, Mark Elder, Antonia Malchik, Leonard Nash, John Keahey, Olivia Raths, John Dufresne, Patsy Mennuti, Alexandra Roland, Jean Paul, John Poppy, Beth Lotspeich, Luisella Romeo, Josh Lieberman, Katarzyna Nowak, and Gilbert Wong. David Beaty and Dave Wieczorek have given me the joy of many bookish conversations and, along with it, inspiration.

My family has always been there for me: my brothers and sisters-in-law—Bill & Pat, Jim & Joyce—and especially my mother, Winifred, who has been reading me longer than anyone. Of course this book—this life—would not have been possible without the inspiring and entertaining presence of Hania.